TIME

HORSES TO FOLLOW

2020/21 JUMPS SEASON

CONTENTS

TIMEFORM

ISBN 978-1-8380349-0-0 Price £10.95

Printed and bound by
Charlesworth Press,
Wakefield, UK 01924 204830

SECTION 1

Timeform's Fifty To Follow, carefully chosen by members of Timeform's editorial staff, are listed below with their respective page numbers. A selection of ten (**marked in bold with a ★**) is made for those who prefer a smaller list.

The form summary for each horse is shown after its age, colour, sex and pedigree. The summary shows the distance, the state of the going and where the horse finished in each of its races since the start of the 2019/20 season. Performances are in chronological sequence with the date of its last race shown at the end (F-ran on Flat).

The distance of each race is given in furlongs. Steeplechase form figures are prefixed by the letter 'c', hurdle form figures by the letter 'h' and NH Flat race or bumper form figures by the letter 'b'.

The going is symbolised as follows: f–firm, m–good to firm; g–good, d–good to soft; s–soft; v–heavy.

Placings are indicated, up to the sixth place, by use of superior figures, an asterisk being used to denote a win and superior letters are used to convey what happened to a horse during the race: F–fell, pu–pulled up, ur–unseated rider, bd–brought down, su–slipped up, ro–ran out.

The Timeform Rating of a horse is simply the merit of the horse expressed in pounds and is arrived at by careful examination of its running against other horses. The ratings range from 175+ for the champions down to a figure of around 55 for selling platers. Symbols attached to the ratings: 'p'–likely to improve; 'P'–capable of much better form; '+'–the horse may be better than we have rated it.

Adrimel (Fr) b111

5 b.g. Tirwanako (Fr) – Irise de Gene (Fr) (Blushing Flame (USA))
2019/20 b15.8v* b16.6s* b16.4s Mar 11

Assessing trainer performance purely by P/L over a period of time fails to provide results of much worth. For instance, of the jumps trainers who have saddled 100 runners or more in the UK over the last six seasons, Gail Haywood is clear at the top of the list with a profit of £139.50 (to a £1 level stake) courtesy of winners at 40/1 and two at 80/1. And even Gail's most ardent fan would struggle to convince many that it's a yard generally worth following, acknowledging they deserve credit for winning eight races during that time given the average Timeform rating of their runners was a little over 70. By contrast, Ruth Jefferson sits fourth in that table with a level-stake profit of £63.50 and the average rating of her runners was almost 30 lb higher.

One trainer who shows up notably well using a range of metrics is Tom Lacey. Not only do his runners show a level-stake profit, but he's also in the top 10 so far as strike rate is concerned and figures prominently using the Run To Form and Impact Value metrics, too. Essentially, Lacey is very good at placing his horses, though it's unlikely he'll have to think too hard about where he runs Adrimel in the first instance next season, as winning a maiden/novice hurdle will be little more than a formality judged on the useful level of form he showed in bumpers. He was the wide-margin winner of a small-field affair at Uttoxeter first time up before posting an effort with much more substance at Doncaster a couple of months later, conceding a penalty to The Edgar Wallace (successful next time out) with the pair a long way clear. Adrimel failed to cut any ice in the Champion Bumper on his final outing, doing plenty up with the pace before dropping away, but he did impress with his physique beforehand, maybe unsurprisingly given he cost the princely sum of £280,000 after winning a two-finisher event on his sole start in Irish points. ***Tom Lacey***

Conclusion: ***Adrimel has all the ingredients to develop into a useful novice hurdler in 2020/21 and, with his trainer's record, it's safe to assume he'll have a campaign mapped out long before he steps on to the track for his hurdling debut***

Albert's Back **c127p**

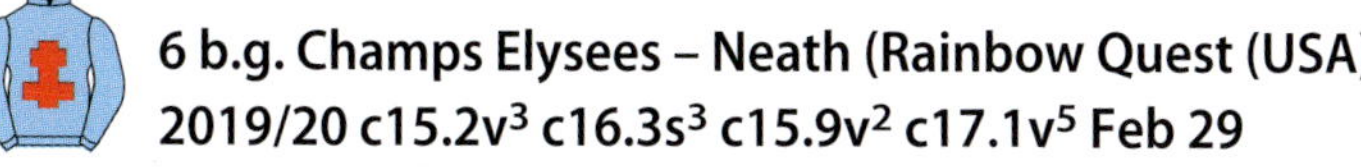

6 b.g. Champs Elysees – Neath (Rainbow Quest (USA))
2019/20 c15.2v^3 c16.3s^3 c15.9v^2 c17.1v^5 Feb 29

On the face of it, the inclusion of Albert's Back in the *Fifty* could be deemed surprising. After all, he's had four goes over fences without winning and was notably disappointing on the last of those runs. But there have been extenuating circumstances on occasions, his jumping has largely impressed, and he's still got plenty of time on his side, only six and with a mere seven races over jumps under his belt, too.

Albert's Back certainly showed plenty of promise on his first two stabs at chasing. He jumped accurately when chasing home the useful pair Good Boy Bobby and Ravenhill Road at Wetherby, and he again looked assured over fences when not beaten far in a tactical small-field affair at Newcastle, the pair who beat him that day both successful next time out. He had no chance with the smart First Flow at Leicester next time then was easy to back when flopping in a handicap at Kelso on his final outing. All four outings over fences have been on soft or heavy going and, whilst acknowledging that conditions were soft when Albert's Back won his first two races over hurdles at Wetherby, it would hardly be surprising if less testing conditions see this Flat-bred to better advantage, especially given his speed and nimble jumping. ***Michael Easterby***

Conclusion: ***2m handicap chases are often less competitive than might be expected, especially in the North, and Albert's Back showed enough in his first season over fences to believe he'll be able to capitalise on a potentially lenient mark next time round***

Simon Walker (Albert's Back): *"A good mark coupled with a bit of improvement can often take a horse a long way in 2m handicap chases in the North – Nuts Well was a good example in 2019/20 – and Albert's Back is just the sort of lightly-raced chaser to make hay in his second season over fences, lots of options for him given that he's still a novice, too."*

Aye Right (Ire) c141

7 b.g. Yeats (Ire) – Gaybric (Ire) (Presenting)
2019/20 h20.9g* h20s^{2} c24v^{ur} c23.4s* c24.4s^{5} Mar 11

Harriet Graham is a rather unique figure in British racing in that she combines being a clerk of the course with training from her base near Jedburgh in the Scottish Borders. Musselburgh, one of the tracks at which she is clerk, has faced plenty of challenges with regards its future in recent years, but one future that does look pretty certain is that of Graham's star horse Aye Right.

Winner of five of his 12 hurdle starts and second a further five times, he's a really likeable performer who took his form up even further when sent chasing mid-way through last season. Having been in the process of making an encouraging debut over fences when unseating at the thirteenth in the Grade 2 December Novice's Chase at Doncaster, he made no mistake when readily accounting for his sole rival Mulcahys Hill at Newcastle next time.

Two very small-field novice events left him short on experience pitched into the RSA Chase at Cheltenham and that inexperience did rather catch him out, a couple of sizeable mistakes hindering his chance, but despite that he was still in touch three fences from home and acquitted himself about as well as could have been expected in the circumstances. Being in the cut and thrust of such a hot race should really have helped put a competitive edge on him as a chaser, and he has the tools to progress again this season. A BHA mark of 146 is likely to be exploitable in the North, with races like the Rehearsal Chase at Newcastle and the Rowland Meyrick at Wetherby sure to come under consideration—indeed, there is a certain similarity between himself and Top Ville Ben who won the latter of those races having shaped best when a close third in the former last season. ***Harriet Graham***

Conclusion: *Admirable sort who took well to chasing in a trio of outings last season. The experience gained in a very competitive RSA shouldn't be lost on him and he has the scope to land a big staying handicap in the North*

Bear Ghylls (Ire) b105+

5 br.g. Arcadio (Ger) – Inch Princess (Ire) (Oscar (Ire))
2019/20 b16v* Mar 8

Nicky Martin hasn't had an entrant in our *Fifty* before now but she's a trainer who has been quietly impressing for some time, her small string—all of them wearing the colours of the Bradley Partnership—including likeable types such as The Two Amigos and Sykes, who she has managed to improve from David Pipe and Philip Hobbs respectively.

However, there's a chance that Bear Ghylls could just be the best she's had, such was the impression he created on debut at Warwick in early-March. The race in question clearly fell apart to an extent, the odds-on favourite Your Darling one of the first beaten, but Bear Ghylls—an attractive sort in the paddock—could hardly have been more impressive in beating the rest, powering through the race and breaking his rivals one by one at the end of the back straight. The timefigure adds substance to the style (overall time compared favourably with the opening novice hurdle on the card) and Bear Ghylls is an exciting hurdling prospect, one who is likely to stay beyond 2m, from the family of the Nicky Richards-trained Merrydown, a fellow first-time-out bumper winner who was successful in two novice hurdles before finishing sixth in the Grade 1 Sefton Novices' Hurdle. ***Nicky Martin***

Conclusion: *Wildly impressive debut bumper winner who looks a smart hurdling prospect for his underrated yard*

Brinkley (Fr) h135p

5 gr.g. Martaline – Royale Majesty (Fr) (Nikos)
2019/20 b16.5s h20.2s^3 h20.5s* Feb 28

David Pipe has history with French-bred greys. Think Grands Crus, Dynaste and Ramses de Teillee, whose three wins in 2019/20 included two Grade 2 novice hurdles. Last season was a resurgent one for the stable in general, an impressive 19% strike-rate underpinned by more advanced metrics that show their runners often outperformed market expectations. Brinkley, who shares his sire with Dynaste and Ramses de Teillee, did his bit for that stat when scoring on his only outing for Pipe in a novice hurdle at Newbury in February, and we're anticipating big things from him in 2020/21.

Formerly trained in Ireland by Liz Doyle, Brinkley lined up at Newbury with a promising third in a well-contested maiden hurdle at Punchestown under his belt, and he built significantly on that to open his account, powering clear and recording a useful effort supported by a good timefigure. There was talk of Cheltenham in the aftermath, but it's no bad thing that he swerved the Festival, not least as it protected a generous-looking opening BHA mark of 130. Connections will surely be rubbing their hands at the thought of exploiting that in 2020/21, and the valuable 3m handicap hurdle on Betfair Chase day at Haydock—a race the Pipe stable has often targeted, winning it with the grey trio Grands Crus, Dynaste and Gevrey Chambertin—could well be on the agenda, the way Brinkley finished at Newbury suggesting he'll relish a step up in trip. ***David Pipe***

Conclusion: *Lightly-raced type who impressed when wide-margin winner of Newbury novice on only outing for current stable; opening mark looks lenient on that bare form, and has plenty of scope for further improvement, especially up at 3m*

Simon Baker (Brinkley): *"If Brinkley is as good as he looked when winning at Newbury then he'll prove an opening mark of 130 to be a total rick. Beyond that, his lightly-raced profile, physique, pedigree, and as-yet-untapped stamina add up to one of the most compelling overall packages in this season's Fifty".*

Chantry House (Ire) h144

6 br.g. Yeats (Ire) – The Last Bank (Ire) (Phardante (Fr))
2019/20 h16.8s* h16.3g* h16.4s^3 Mar 10

The previous three renewals of the Supreme—won by Labaik (2017), Summerville Boy (2018) and Klassical Dream (2019)—haven't produced quite the same calibre of horse as some of the renewals in the early/mid-2010s, in which the likes of Sprinter Sacre, Cue Card, My Tent or Yours, Jezki, Vautour, Douvan, Sizing John, Altior, Min and Buveur d'Air all either won or made the frame before scaling even greater heights, but there's definite hope that the latest renewal will yield a superstar or two.

The winner Shishkin was one of the first names on the teamsheet for this year's *Fifty*, but the third place Chantry House is another superb novice chasing prospect for current champion trainer Nicky Henderson. Both are chasing types in appearance and background (point winners) and, though Chantry House is hardly slow—he won

Chantry House (right) looks a smart prospect for novice chasing

a bumper and two steadily-run novice hurdles before placing in the Supreme—he is seemingly the stronger stayer of the pair, perhaps likely to have shown up in the Baring Bingham at Cheltenham instead had owner J.P. McManus not had Sporting John for that race. Given his pedigree (by Yeats and related to plenty of 2½m winners on the dam's side) and how he's viewed by his connections, it's probably to Chantry House's credit that he got up into the mid-140s on ratings running solely over 2m. He looks set to be campaigned over a bit further when sent chasing (which will also mean he avoids the speedier Shishkin) and could make up into a leading contender for the Golden Miller this season, also worth noting how well his half-brother The Last Day took to chasing (rated 124 over hurdles and 141 over fences). ***Nicky Henderson***

Conclusion: *Quickly made up into a useful novice hurdler at 2m last season despite lacking a change of gear in the Supreme; smart prospect for novice chasing at 2½m*

Clondaw Caitlin (Ire) h130p

5 b.m. Court Cave (Ire) – Kilmessan (Ire) (Flemensfirth (USA))
2019/20 b17d b16s* h19.7v* h20.3s* h18.1v* Feb 29

It can be as much a curse as a blessing to follow a successful parent into the same line of work. For every Angelina Jolie, Ben Stiller and Stuart Broad, whose fame and achievements are arguably greater than those of their father, there have been those who enjoyed some success in their own right but still suffer by comparison. See the likes of Jordi Cruyff, Alan Berry and either of John Lennon's sons. Ruth Jefferson falls somewhere in between those two stools. She took over from her father after he enjoyed a great career, and though she has a far smaller team than Malcolm at the height of his success, she's still a force to be reckoned with, as touched upon in the piece on Adrimel.

In Clondaw Caitlin she has an exciting prospect on her hands. Winner of a Wetherby bumper on her second start, she then went unbeaten in three novice hurdles, ready wins back at Wetherby and Newcastle followed by quite a smooth success against geldings in the Grade 2 Premier Novices' Hurdle at Kelso. To win a race like that over 2¼m bodes particularly well as she's bred to appreciate a good bit further (her dam, unraced herself, comes from a strong staying family).

With that in mind, Clondaw Caitlin has plenty of options this season, particularly over 2½m and further, the good series of graded mares' hurdles that there is these days catering well for this type of horse. She'll undoubtedly jump a fence in time but is young enough for that to be on the back burner for now, and she has major pretensions of taking the mantle of the best mare in the North from an ageing Lady Buttons this season. ***Ruth Jefferson***

Conclusion: ***Won four races in her first season under Rules, including all three over hurdles, and has definite scope to progress further, particularly as her stamina is drawn out***

Coeur Serein (Ire) h113p

6 b.g. Fame And Glory – Balvenie (Ire) (Oscar (Ire))
2019/20 b20.9g^3 b16s^3 h16d h20.5s^3 h19.7v^2 Mar 17

Coueur Serein is one of the lowest-rated horses in this edition of the *Fifty*, but we'd be disappointed if he hasn't improved his rating significantly by the end of the season, hopefully having picked up a few handicaps along the way. After all, there's been obvious promise in each of his five outings under Rules so far despite none of them really having got to the bottom of him.

A staying-on third in a Chepstow bumper in November on his first run for Jonjo O'Neill (behind two subsequent hurdles winners, including fellow *Fifty* member Gustavian), Coeur Serein made the places on his second and third outings over timber, and was especially eye-catching doing his best work at the finish when third to Brinkley (also in the *Fifty*) at Newbury in February. Coeur Serein has only raced up to 2½m so far, but he's bred for stamina and shapes that way too, and the chances are that connections have had their eye on staying handicaps for him from the word go. An opening mark of 114 is far from punitive considering the promise he's shown, and a step up to 3m could be just what he needs to show exactly what he can do. ***Jonjo O'Neill***

Conclusion: ***Did good groundwork under patient rides in a trio of novice hurdles and looks just the type to come into his own once upped to 3m and switched to a handicap***

Danny Whizzbang (Ire) c144p

7 b.g. Getaway (Ger) – Lakil Princess (Ire) (Bering)
2019/20 c23.4g* c24s^3 c23.8v^3 Feb 15

There have been a raft of racehorses named after characters from the hit BBC series Peaky Blinders in recent years. We've seen a Tommy Shelby and Thomas Shelby (the show's main character), Aberama Gold (a Romany Gypsy hitman) and, quite possibly the best character in the show, Alfie Solomons (played by Tom Hardy).

The character Danny Whizzbang only appeared in three episodes before being killed by Billy Kimber (a three-year-old trained by Stuart Crawford) but is already the best racehorse of the lot, bursting onto the chasing scene when taking the scalp of dual Grade 1-winning hurdler Reserve Tank in the John Francome Novices' Chase at Newbury in November, looking better the further he went. That took his overall record

Danny Whizzbang tackles the water jump on his way to victory at Newbury

under Rules to three from three (unbeaten in two novice hurdles) and his subsequent two defeats are easy enough to forgive. He was unsettled after being hampered by the fall of his stablemate in the Kauto Star at Kempton and then seemed to find barely-raceable ground against him in the Reynoldstown at Ascot, travelling as well as anything for a long way but weakening from two out and finishing a tired third.

A €115,000 purchase as a five-year-old following a point win, it's easy to see why he fetched so much, a huge, raw type of horse with bags of scope who'll be even better with another summer under his belt. He's likely to make much more of an impact at the highest level in 2020/21 if connections opt to go down that route straight away, but a more patient approach may also pay dividends, his trainer a dab hand at placing second-season chasers in top-end handicaps, with a BHA mark of 145 underplaying his potential.
Paul Nicholls

Conclusion: *Impressive winning chasing debut went unsupported last season but has the raw materials to make up for lost time in 2020/21*

Discko des Plages (Fr) h107 c -p

7 b.g. Balko (Fr) – Lady des Plages (Fr) (Chamberlin (Fr))
2019/20 c19.9s[ur] h16.6d[6] h19.4v* Feb 28

2019/20 was Richard Hobson's most successful season so far, narrowly bettering his previous highest haul of winners and prize money, while his strike rate of 26.53% was the fourth best in the UK of trainers who had at least 25 runners, and this is the first time we've included one of his horses in the *Fifty*. Lord du Mesnil, the stable star, held his form superbly last season, completing a hat-trick in November/December and finishing second on his other four starts, culminating in the National Hunt Chase at Cheltenham. Discko des Plages is nowhere near that level at present but did his bit for the yard's strike rate last season, winning one of his three starts, and he looks set to build on that this time around.

A tall son of Balko, he's all over a chaser in appearance and went over fences last season, though chasing was shelved after he failed to complete on his reappearance, unseating at the last when looking set to fight out fourth in a Huntingdon novice handicap. That was a more encouraging effort than might be suggested from the fact that he went straight back over hurdles, and he seems sure to make a better fist of chasing this campaign with the extra time behind him. He was better than ever when rewarding plenty of support at Doncaster on his final start in the manner of one well ahead of his mark (clear early in the straight), looking well suited by front running, tactics that should stand him in good stead back over fences. He can return to chasing from a mark 3 lb below his revised hurdles one and it will be disappointing if he can't find a race or two in 2020/21. ***Richard Hobson***

Conclusion: *Very well backed prior to winning a Doncaster handicap hurdle in good style when last seen and ought to be able to win races over fences this season*

Easy As That (Ire) b118+

5 b.g. Sans Frontieres (Ire) – Bell Storm (Ire) (Glacial Storm (USA))
2019/20 b15.8v* b16.4s* Feb 18

First-time-out bumper winners aren't quite so rare as might have been expected for Venetia Williams—she's been responsible for eight over the last six seasons—but during that period none had gone on to defy a penalty in another bumper. Until Easy As That that is. And the impression he created when doing so marks him down as a cracking prospect.

The market suggested Easy As That had been showing plenty at home prior to his debut at Ffos Las and, whilst the form wasn't easy to equate, the way he opened up late in the day to win by four lengths was really encouraging. He achieved considerably more when defying a penalty at Musselburgh a couple of months later, again making all and powering away in the straight to win by a wide margin, in the process recording one of the highest bumper figures of the season by a British-trained horse. Encouragingly, the runner-up that day subsequently went on to run another similarly promising type Tupelo Mississippi close at Newcastle a month later. ***Venetia Williams***

Conclusion: *The way the stable operates means that Easy As That is likely to be campaigned as a nascent chaser rather than have a hectic novice hurdle campaign in 2020/21, but the ability he showed in bumpers strongly suggests he'll be capable of useful form at least over the smaller obstacles, several races bound to come his way even if he doesn't end up being regularly campaigned in graded company*

Elf de Re (Fr) h128

6 ch.g. Anabaa Blue – Ninon de Re (Fr) (Denham Red (Fr))
2019/20 h16.2s^3 h16.2v* h22.7v^2 h18.1v^2 Feb 29

"If anyone sees me going anywhere near a boat again they have my permission to shoot me". The actual words quoted are often slightly different but the sentiment was crystal clear—Sir Steve Redgrave had had enough of rowing after winning his fourth Olympic gold medal at Atlanta in 1996. Yet soon after, Redgrave resolved to put himself through another torturous Olympic training regime with the aim of a fifth gold four years later. Jockeys, like rowers, often have to put their bodies through the wringer, and yet many who call it a day are drawn back by the buzz of riding winners. Lester Piggott is perhaps the most famous example, the five years he had out of the saddle between 1985 and 1990 including a year spent at Her Majesty's pleasure for tax fraud. In America, Gary Stevens twice came back from retirement, his return from an eight-year hiatus in 2013 seeing him land the only Breeders' Cup Classic of his career. Recently retired Leighton Aspell's second stint riding (having had nearly two years out) saw him ride back-to-back Grand National winners in 2014 and 2015, the first jockey for over 40 years to achieve that feat, while another Grand National-winning jockey Ryan Mania returned to the saddle last season.

Mania hung up his boots the year after landing the National on Aurora's Encore, citing ongoing weight struggles, but, with a nod towards modern-day nutritional advice, has returned from five years out able to ride at a minimum weight of 10-4. Last season was his best ever in terms of strike rate, too, recording 21 winners from 106 rides, all of them for his stepfather-in-law Sandy Thomson. A total of 12 of those wins (from just 33 rides) came in chases, and that's an angle we're keen to explore as both trainer and jockey fare much better over fences than hurdles. Elf de Re was a progressive novice hurdler for the yard last season, his four runs (all at Kelso), including a wide-margin maiden success and a good second to Clondaw Caitlin (a fellow member of the *Fifty*) in the Grade 2 Premier Novices' Hurdle on his final start, but there's plenty about him, including both his attitude and physique, to think he can make a better chaser, while his dam is a half-sister to Pineau de Re, one of those Aspell-ridden Grand National winners. ***Sandy Thomson***

Conclusion: *Reached a near-useful standard over hurdles but every reason to think he can take his form up a notch or two if sent chasing*

Elusive Belle (Ire) h134

6 b.m. Elusive Pimpernel (USA) – Soviet Belle (Ire) (Soviet Star (USA))
2019/20 h16.3g³ h16s² h16.8d⁵ Mar 13

It's not hard to see how Elusive Belle got her name, a quick glance at her pedigree all that's required, and her inclusion in this book is similarly straightforward. She might not have managed to win last season but she ran fine races on all three starts in really good handicap hurdles. A third on her reappearance in a listed event at Newbury to a pair of stablemates—including Epatante no less—was built on when chasing home Miranda at Kempton at Christmas, an untidy jump at the second last helping to swing things the unexposed winner's way, and that too was a good bit of form, third home Eddiemaurice (who'd won the race the year before) going on to win his following start.

Elusive Belle's only other start came in the County Hurdle at Cheltenham in which she performed very creditably to finish fifth, comfortably best of the home-trained contingent in a race dominated by unexposed Irish horses, unable to go with the principals only after the last. Given that she beat all 12 other British-trained rivals, her BHA mark of 136 still looks a good one, a point she should be able to prove this season, particularly should she shed her tendency to race a bit keenly as she matures. It's suspected that she'll stay over hurdles and take in similar events again this campaign, but she does have the physique to jump fences if that's the path connections want to go down. ***Nicky Henderson***

Conclusion: *Had some strong novice form and ran really well in some hot handicaps last season, with the scope to do even better in similar events as she matures*

Espion (Fr) h122p

6 ch.g. Coastal Path – Toutamie (Fr) (Epalo (Ger))
2019/20 h15.3s⁵ h16v³ h19.9v* Mar 14

Espion is French for spy—hence espionage—but it didn't take any deep undercover work to suggest the horse of that name is one to follow in 2020/21. After all, his first two runs over hurdles came in a couple of the best-contested 2m novices of the pre-Christmas period, and while he lacked the pace to threaten the principals in those, he had running left at the finish both times. That's no surprise given the stamina in his pedigree (his dam is a half-sister to staying chasers L'Ami and Kelami), and, a step up to 2½m for a novice at Uttoxeter in March proved just the ticket, Espion relishing the longer trip as he forged right away from his three rivals late on.

An opening BHA mark of 128 is potentially lenient judged on both that win and his prior third at Sandown, and there's more than one good reason why Espion will improve again. For one thing, he still looked a little green in victory at Uttoxeter, but even more pertinent is that he seems sure to relish stepping up to 3m+. The improvement that comes as his stamina is drawn out can ensure Espion stays ahead of the handicapper, whether he sticks to hurdles or goes chasing—he certainly has the physique to take to fences. ***Philip Hobbs***

Conclusion: *Staying type but hasn't yet had the chance to put his stamina to the test; opening mark of 128 is more than fair on form already in the book, and that's without accounting for the improvement that seems all but assured once he tackles 3m+*

Flinteur Sacre (Fr) b106p

5 b.g. Network (Ger) – Fatima III (Fr) (Bayolidaan (Fr))
2019/20 b16.3s^2 b16d* Feb 7

French-bred broodmare Fatima III has had three of her offspring run under Rules in Britain (her first two foals were cross-country horses in France) and all three have been successful in bumpers. Flinteur Sacre and his nine-year older full-brother Sprinter Sacre are the most recent two, but not many racing fans would remember the first without a bit of research. Indeed, Nicky Henderson, J.P. McManus and us at Timeform will be hoping Flinteur Sacre takes to obstacles a fair bit better than Regain du Charbonneau, who went badly the wrong way from his winning debut, ending his career finishing tailed off in a chase at Newton Abbott off a BHA mark of 85.

That said, both of Flinteur Sacre's bumper starts suggest he's a lot more like his illustrious sibling than Regain du Charbonneau ever was, impressing with the way he travelled on debut at Newbury (when second) and then blowing away lesser opposition at Kempton three weeks later. Though his Newbury conqueror Your Darling bombed out next time (like many from the Ben Pauling yard in 2019/20), there's a suspicion that both are well-above-average sorts and Flinteur Sacre (who was reportedly being aimed at the Grade 2 Aintree bumper before the season was cut short) is a really exciting jumping recruit for his top connections. ***Nicky Henderson***

Conclusion: *Cut from the same cloth as one of the best ever and certainly looked the part in two bumper starts last season, clearly a smart prospect for 2m novice hurdles*

Galice Macalo (Fr) h116p

4 b.f. Saddler Maker (Ire) – Victoire de Forme (Fr) (Sabrehill (USA))
2019/20 h16.3g^4 h17s^F h16.6d^6 Jan 24

Galice Macalo might not be a household name just yet but her inclusion in the *Fifty* looks entirely justified. An encouraging debut in a juvenile hurdle at Stratford last July was set to be built on emphatically in a fillies' listed event at Aintree next time when she crashed out at the final flight. Having been a bit keen out the back, she made powerful headway around the outside into the straight to lead two out and was still in front and yet to be asked for anything like full effort when stepping at the last.

Herself and Midnights' Gift had already come clear at that stage and it's encouraging that that filly improved next time against her elders, when chasing home the very promising Marie's Rock at Taunton, especially as Galice Macalo has the greater potential, a jumps bred who was unraced on the Flat and was a bigger sort physically than most juvenile fillies.

She had one further start last season in a similar event at Doncaster but that didn't see her to best effect at all, held up in a race run in a far slower time to the third last than the other 2m races on the card, whilst she also met trouble and showed her inexperience when hanging left away from the whip in the latter stages. She shapes like she'll relish a strong pace and a BHA mark of 120 looks like it could underrate her by a fair way in the right circumstances. A well-run 2m handicap would make her very interesting, while there's every chance from her pedigree that she'll stay a bit further in due course as she settles down, and given she didn't win last season, she remains a novice which is something that connections may well be keen to exploit at some stage, too. ***Jane Williams***

Conclusion: *Likely to have won a listed juvenile fillies' event at Aintree on her second start but for falling late and still has plenty of scope heading into her second season, with a mark of 120 looking very exploitable for handicaps*

Goshen (Fr) h161p

4 b.g. Authorized (Ire) – Hyde (Fr) (Poliglote)
2019/20 h17.7v* h16s* h15.7s* h16.8d^{ur} Mar 13

10 is a very important number in many walks of life beyond its obvious significance in the age of decimalisation. Think the Commandments and the Prime Minister's residence, as well as numerous scoring systems. In sport alone, professional boxing, 10-pin bowling, archery and gymnastics all use 10 as a score that can't be bettered and which sometimes signifies perfection (take Nadia Comăneci's display at the Olympic Games), and it can be

Goshen has the potential to go to the very top over hurdles

taken as a measure of excellence with Goshen too, as that's the distance we think he'd have won the Triumph Hurdle by last season but for departing at the final flight.

His jumping had been widely questioned in the lead-up to the race but, ironically, he'd produced his own nigh-on perfect performance up until there was a misunderstanding between horse and rider at the last. A wide-margin winner of his first three starts over hurdles, he'd jumped right when winning at Fontwell (in particular) and in the latter stages at Ascot but jumped seven of the eight hurdles in the Triumph far better than previously. Indeed, the way he barely broke stride over the tricky second last—a flight that virtually no other member of the field took fluently—suggests there's no long-term issue with his jumping whatsoever. Having surged clear of Allmankind into the straight and been brought across to the near rail, he paddled through the final hurdle but even then the partnership might well have remained intact had his near hind not clamped onto his near fore for a stride, causing the horse to become unbalanced.

A figure of 161 has been bettered only by the ill-fated Our Conor's 15-length Triumph romp by a juvenile in recent memory. In fact, that figure was only bettered by Sharjah's runner-up effort in the Champion Hurdle in the list of Timeform ratings over hurdles in the UK in 2019/20, so there's no doubt that Goshen is a hugely exciting prospect for open graded hurdles this season. Yes, four-going-on-five-year-olds tend to struggle against their elders but Espoir d'Allen struck a blow for the five-year-olds in the Champion Hurdle in 2019 and Goshen is a horse of extraordinary ability—if he had indeed won the Triumph by 10 lengths he'd have won seven in a row, Flat and jumps combined, by an average of more than 15 lengths. He handles testing ground really well but proved in the Triumph that he's equally at home under less testing conditions. He shouldn't have an issue with 2½m either, so the Ascot Hurdle, appeals as a suitable starting point, presuming connections aren't tempted to take advantage of a Flat mark of 88 beforehand, with a Champion Hurdle campaign surely on the cards. ***Gary Moore***

Conclusion: *Would have made it seven in a row over Flat and jumps combined, all by wide margins, had he not unshipped his jockey at the final flight in the Triumph and looks as exciting a horse stepping out of juvenile hurdling company as there's been for many years*

Gustavian (Ire) h116p

5 b.g. Mahler – Grange Oscar (Ire) (Oscar (Ire))
2019/20 b16s^2 b15.8v^2 h16.8v* h19.9v^2 Mar 14

Of the trainers who have sent out more than 200 runners in handicap hurdles in the UK over the last six seasons only two have a better strike rate than Anthony Honeyball, the Dorset trainer also faring well in other metrics such as P/L and 'Run To Form' in the same category. There's a good chance Gustavian will be doing his bit to at least maintain Honeyball's excellent record in handicap hurdles in 2020/21, the five-year-old doing more than enough in a couple of bumpers and his first two starts over hurdles to think that an opening BHA mark of 120 is on the lenient side.

Gustavian was set an awful lot to do when runner-up in bumpers at Chepstow and Ffos Las before being ridden much more prominently when making a successful start over hurdles in a maiden at Exeter, impressively strong at the finish that day. It was rather surprising, therefore, that patient tactics were readopted when upped in trip for his next outing, Gustavian clearly not seen to best advantage in a small-field novice at Uttoxeter won by fellow member of the *Fifty* Espion. Gustavian should be fully effective over at least 2½m and has raced solely on soft or heavy going to date. ***Anthony Honeyball***

Conclusion: *Some horses give the impression they'll be seen to much better advantage in handicaps than maidens/novices and Gustavian most definitely falls into that category, his trainer a dab hand at making the most of potentially lenient opening marks*

Dan Barber (Gustavian): *"Had Gustavian been ridden as close to the pace as he was when winning an Exeter maiden on his hurdling debut on his other three starts, he'd likely be entering his second season defending an unbeaten four-from-four record. He can surely make amends in 2020/21—he retains significant potential and will be starting life in handicaps from a generous-looking mark."*

Happygolucky (Ire) h135

6 br.g. Jeremy (USA) – Mydadsabishop (Ire) (Bishop of Cashel)
2019/20 h22s* h21v³ h19.8s³ h20.3d⁴ Mar 13

Over the last five seasons the average Kim Bailey-trained hurdler has achieved a peak Timeform rating of 96.7, while his average chaser is rated 113.8, an improvement of just over a stone. Those figures won't surprise many given the type of horse Bailey has become known for in recent seasons—straightforward and tough front-running chasers. The likes of Imperial Aura (h132p c153p), First Flow (h137 c148), Two For Gold (h126p c144) and Newtide (h132 c140) all took significant steps forward during their novice chasing campaigns last season and Happygolucky—like the last-named owned by Lady Dulverton—looks highly likely to do the same in 2020/21. A rangy type who finished runner-up on his sole start in Irish points, Happygolucky looked useful from day one under Rules, staying on strongly to win a maiden at Stratford on debut. He backed that effort up by making the frame on his subsequent three starts in the Hyde, Winter Hurdle and Martin Pipe, doing particularly well on the last occasion considering his relative inexperience. If improving in line with similar types from his yard, he should make up into a smart chaser next season, particularly with a view to stepping up in trip. ***Kim Bailey***

Conclusion: ***Reached a useful level over hurdles in just four starts, coping notably well in the Martin Pipe given his inexperience, and seems sure to improve for the switch to fences/step up to 3m+, races like the Towton at Wetherby likely to be on his agenda this season***

Highland Hunter (Ire) h130p

7 gr.g. Subtle Power (Ire) – Loughine Sparkle (Ire) (Beneficial)
2019/20 h24.3d h26.1s* Feb 2

The North-South divide is a factor in nearly all walks of life and the fact that Paul Nicholls is the fourth most successful trainer at Musselburgh in the past five seasons despite training around 400 miles south of the course only goes to highlight the region-based disparity in the sphere of National Hunt racing. Nicholls has achieved this feat (17 winners) from just 39 runners, a strike-rate of 43.6%, a startling figure considering the track's leading trainer in that timeframe, Lucinda Russell, has 33 winners from some 255 tries. Though it obviously detracts from the sport as a whole, it's easy to see why owners like Thomas Barr move their horses down South to the powerhouse yards of Nicholls and Henderson, and unfortunately for Russell, that's just what happened with Highland Hunter after 2018/19.

After shaping as if in need of the outing on reappearance at Haydock, Highland Hunter was very strong in the betting in Musselburgh's Pertemps Network qualifier in February and duly landed the odds, a fairly narrow winning margin from one of his former stablemates, Mighty Thunder, not telling the full story, Harry Cobden very cool in the saddle as he got his mount in front close home. Things might not have gone to plan with Highland Hunter afterwards (that run qualified him for the Pertemps Final at Cheltenham but he was taken out of the race later that month), but he's still likely to be of plenty of interest in the coming season, either kept to hurdles or if switched to fences, the type to make a chaser (point winner) and still very lightly raced for a superb yard. ***Paul Nicholls***

Conclusion: *Only two starts over hurdles for Paul Nicholls and this strong-travelling type remains with untapped potential heading into 2020/21*

Highway One O Two (Ire) h139p

5 b.g. Shirocco (Ger) – Supreme Dreamer (Ire) (Supreme Leader)
2019/20 b16.3d2 b15.7s4 h15.9s* h15.9s* h16s* Feb 22

Last season was the first time we've included Chris Gordon-trained horses in the *Fifty*, and it didn't go well, with Baddesley Prince failing to appear and Shut The Box soon stalling after a good start. The fault lies with us though, as it was another fine season for the upwardly-mobile Gordon team. On The Slopes and Commanche Red were both good winners we could conceivably have uncovered instead, though it's forgivable that we missed out on the star performer Highway One O Two. After all, there was only minor promise in his two bumper runs early in 2019, but after an unbeaten first season over timber, including a Grade 2, we're very keen to have him on our side this time round.

Highway One O Two had a couple more tries in bumpers earlier last season, and while he didn't get his head in front, he shaped well both times and had obviously come back an improved model. Even so, it was a bit surprising to see him take quite so well to hurdling, twice demolishing his rivals in 2m novices at Plumpton before heading to Kempton for the Dovecote, where he was again full of enthusiasm and never saw another rival. There was talk afterwards of the Top Novices' Hurdle at Aintree (a mark of 145 made the Imperial Cup less appealing) but with that fixture abandoned it'll be a quick switch to chasing for Highway One O Two. That's an exciting proposition, as his zestful, forward-going style promises to make him a sight to behold over fences. If he takes to it as well as we think, further graded race success will surely be on the cards. ***Chris Gordon***

Conclusion: *Impressive every time when going unbeaten in first season over hurdles and looks tailor-made to prove even better over fences*

Hold The Note (Ire) c146

6 b.g. Jeremy (USA) – Keys Hope (Ire) (Luso)
2019/20 c20v^{3} c20.5s^{pu} c24s^{2} c20.2s^{3} Mar 10

Having winners at both the Cheltenham Festival and Royal Ascot isn't as rare as you might think. Since 2000, 22 trainers have had at least one winner at each meeting, while eight have managed two or more, the most impressive numbers belonging to Wille Mullins, who has trained six Royal Ascot winners in that period to go with his 67 Cheltenham. For a long time, it would've been difficult to envisage Mick Channon joining the list given he focused nearly entirely on the Flat, but the stable has had a select band of jumpers since joining forces with the retiring Henrietta Knight in 2012, and Mister Whitaker's win in the 2018 Close Brothers Novices' Handicap Chase provided the stable with its first Festival winner. Channon has had live chances at jumping's showpiece in both seasons since, and though Hold The Note only managed third in the most recent renewal of the Close Brothers (now the Northern Trust), we firmly believe there are some good races in him.

In common with most of Channon's jumpers in the Tim Radford colours, Hold The Note is a chasing type who jumps well, and though he didn't win in his first season over fences, he quickly established himself as a smart and likeable performer. The form of his final two runs in particular reads well, just getting outstayed when second in a 3m Grade 2 novice at Warwick in January prior to that third in the Northren Trust—surely one of the strongest handicap chases of the entire season—in which a bit of trouble before the home turn stopped him making even more of an impact. That's more than enough to suggest Hold The Note is well treated, and a return to Cheltenham in the autumn for the BetVictor could well be on the cards, though the fact he retains his novice status means connections have a wide range of options open to them. ***Mick Channon***

Conclusion: *Reached a high level of form in first season over fences despite going winless, signing off with a third in a red-hot handicap; looks an ideal type for valuable handicaps up to 3m, though good novices will also be an option*

Imperial Alcazar (Ire) h138p

6 b.g. Vinnie Roe (Ire) – Maddy's Supreme (Ire) (Supreme Leader)
2019/20 h20d* h22v^{2} h20.3s^{2} h20.5v* Jan 29

By just about every measure 2019/2020 was an outstanding season for Fergal O'Brien. With 63 winners on the board at a 19% clip, it was his best campaign numerically, and, but for its premature end, it could well have been the best in terms of prize money as well. More sophisticated measures back up those impressive basic numbers, and among trainers who sent out more than 100 runners, O'Brien features in the top 10 for impact value and percentage of rivals beaten, his runners also returning a whopping 135-point profit at Betfair SP.

Imperial Alcazar contributed two wins to his yard's tally in his first season over hurdles, bookending the campaign with success at Aintree and Leicester, though there was a brief period where it was three, the raceday stewards awarding him a listed novice at Cheltenham on New Year's Day before first-past-the-post Protekorat was reinstated on appeal. That's a very solid piece of form, as are Imperial Alcazar's other three efforts, and it's probably the least of his ability considering he's a staying type who's yet to get the chance to tackle 3m. It's no bad thing for his long-term development that he swerved the Cheltenham Festival, and chasing will probably be on the agenda for 2020/21. Imperial Alcazar certainly has the physique for that job and, if all goes well, there's little doubt he's got the makings of a smart staying novice. ***Fergal O'Brien***

Conclusion: *Plenty of substance to the useful form achieved in his first season over timber and every indication that he'll make an even better chaser, especially once tackling staying trips*

Imperial Aura (Ire) c153p

7 b.g. Kalanisi (Ire) – Missindependence (Ire) (Executive Perk)
2019/20 h19.5s³ c24.2d* c25.3s² c20.6s² c20.2s* Mar 10

Trainer Harry Whittington and owners Andrew and Kate Brooks must have experienced a mixture of pride and frustration in seeing Saint Calvados go so close to giving them a first Cheltenham Festival winner in the Ryanair last season. They didn't have to wait long for that first success however, Simply The Betts going one better in the Plate two races later. The latter had beaten Imperial Aura in a particularly strong edition of the Timeform Novices' Handicap Chase on Trials Day, that horse going on to provide his own trainer Kim Bailey with a significant success at Cheltenham—his first at the Festival since Darna five years earlier—and he was visibly emotional in a post-race interview. Both Simply The Betts and Imperial Aura have upwards of 10 lb further improvement to find to get to the level of the aforementioned Saint Calvados, but both look capable of making their mark at open graded level this season, with our preference for a spot in this book lying with Imperial Aura.

We try not to include the same horses in the *Fifty* in consecutive years but the case for Imperial Aura is a very strong one. He's improved with virtually every run of his life and barely missed a beat in seeing off the Gordon Elliott-trained Galvin in the Northern Trust at Cheltenham, the pair of them drawing well clear from what had been a still-packed field three out. Having been raised to a mark of 157 handicaps may well be off the agenda now, but that needn't stop Imperial Aura's progression. Mister Whitaker,

Imperial Aura (right) on his way to victory at the Cheltenham Festival

the 2018 winner of the novices' handicap chase at Cheltenham, made a winning reappearance the following season in the Colin Parker Memorial Intermediate Chase and that contest looks a good starting point for Imperial Aura, Bailey having had five winners from nine runners at Carlisle over the past five years, a higher strike rate than at any other course. The Peterborough Chase at Huntingdon (a race Bailey won with Charbel in 2018) is a contest that may well be high on his agenda afterwards, and, with a dearth of obvious home-trained contenders for the Ryanair at present (the first three home in the Marsh are all trained in Ireland, for instance), he could well develop into the leading British-trained contender for that race come March. ***Kim Bailey***

Conclusion: ***Very impressive in seeing off a fellow strongly-backed rival in winning at Cheltenham and could well make up into a genuine Ryanair candidate***

It's Probably Me — h122p

5 b.m. Great Pretender (Ire) – Sting In The Gale (Scorpion (Ire))
2019/20 b16.7g^{2} b16.4v^{5} h18.9s^{ur} h16.5s^{3} h21s^{2} h19.4v* Feb 28

Henry Daly might not have the ammunition he once did but a pair of places from just a handful of runners at the Cheltenham Festival last season shows that he can still be competitive in the big races. Having kept plenty of horses fresh for spring campaigns—neither of the duo who were placed at Cheltenham had run previously in the calendar year—Daly will no doubt be ruing the premature end to the season more than most, particularly as in It's Probably Me he had a mare who looked likely to run a big race in her intended spring target, presumably the Mares' Final at Newbury.

The upshot of the season finishing early is that she's a well-handicapped mare heading into this campaign, a BHA mark of 122 looking a tidy one judged on any of her three completed starts over hurdles (likewise her bumper form). Understandably no match for Marie's Rock faced with a test of speed over 2m at Taunton, she wasn't seen to as good effect as the winner Molly Ollys Wishes at Warwick on her next start, forced wide when that one was able to save ground, and comfortably reversed the form at Doncaster afterwards, her jockey not having to pick up his stick.

She's got the scope and pedigree to jump fences (has looked a pretty accurate jumper since unseating at the first on her hurdling debut) but she's only five-going-on-six and has unfinished business over hurdles in the meantime, easy to see her winning a mares' handicap or two. ***Henry Daly***

Conclusion: ***A bumper winner who really got the hang of hurdling after an early mishap on debut, she looks open to further progress and a handicap is likely to be well within range from her current mark, that she's proved herself on a variety of different grounds a positive for her inclusion in this book***

Land of Winter (Fr) h108p

4 b.g. Camelot – Gaselee (USA) (Toccet (USA))

2019/20 h15.8v^3 h15.8s^2 Mar 11

Rae Guest has very few runners over jumps. In fact, prior to Land of Winter making his hurdling debut in February 2020, he'd had just three other runners over hurdles, namely his first ever winner Run Free in 1989, dual winner Lastroseofsummer in 2010/11 and The Eagle's Nest in early-2019. There was more than enough encouragement in Land of Winter's two efforts over timber, however, to suggest he's almost certainly got a long-term future in the sphere.

Land of Winter was steadily progressive at an ordinary level on the Flat in 2019, winning a handicap at Southwell (from a BHA mark of 51) by a wide margin then going on to show better form in defeat from higher marks in the autumn, displaying considerable reserves of stamina into the bargain. His two runs over hurdles were both at the minimum trip and on each occasion he left the strong impression that he'll be very well suited by a greater emphasis on stamina, which is hardly surprising given his Flat profile. Nevertheless, a couple of placed efforts were enough to qualify him for a mark and it's reasonable to assume he's open to a fair amount of improvement over longer distances. ***Rae Guest***

Conclusion: *It's possible that Land of Winter will mix Flat and hurdling over the next couple of years but, whilst his potential for the former is probably limited, there's a good chance he'll be able to improve for some time yet as a hurdler, especially as his stamina gets tested further*

Marie's Rock (Ire) h140P

5 b.m. Milan – By The Hour (Ire) (Flemensfirth (USA))
2019/20 b15.8g* h15.7d* h16.5s* Dec 30

It's a real pity that injury ruled Marie's Rock out of the Cheltenham Festival, as the impression she'd created when winning her first three starts was enough to think she'd have been the leading home-trained contender for the Dawn Run. Her Timeform rating after just two runs over hurdles is higher than that of every horse who ran in that race bar the winner Concertista, and the large P attached to it denotes that we reckon she's capable of significant further improvement. If we're right about that, then Marie's Rock seems sure to make up for lost time in 2020/21.

The hallmark of Marie's Rock's three wins, comprising a bumper at Ffos Las, an introductory hurdle at Haydock and a listed mares' novice at Taunton, has been a sharp turn of foot in the closing stages, and it's not as if she wasn't beating anything either, the form of her Haydock win against males in particular having been well advertised since. That change of pace is all the more remarkable considering Marie's Rock is bred to stay 2½m+. Indeed, she'll probably make a chaser in time, but there's no hurry to head that way just yet, and there's a strong programme of listed and graded mares' hurdles that should enable her to make hay. ***Nicky Henderson***

Conclusion: *Bundles of promise when going unbeaten in injury-curtailed first season and surely a matter of time before she's winning graded races confined to her own sex*

Marown (Ire) h132p

6 b.g. Milan – Rosie Suspect (Ire) (Presenting)
2019/20 h20.5v* h20.5v* Mar 7

Marown shares his name with a parish on the Isle of Man, where his owner Trevor Hemmings lives, and he's typical of the type of horse Hemmings buys in that he's got the looks and pedigree of a staying chaser. With that in mind, it's especially encouraging that he's gone unbeaten in a bumper and two hurdles—he's very much one to follow in 2020/21 and, all being well, beyond.

Bought for €80,000 as a three-year-old, it's no surprise that Nicky Richards has been in no hurry with Marown, and it wasn't until March 2019 that he made his debut in a bumper at Newcastle, when getting up late to land a race that's since been well advertised over hurdles. It wasn't far off 10 months before Marown had his attentions switched that way, and he overcame greenness to get the better of a next-time winner in a 2½m maiden at Ayr. He returned to the same course and distance for his only other outing and put up his most polished effort yet when powering clear late to defy a penalty at the expense of useful chaser Aloomomo.

Marown will surely be chasing himself in 2020/21 and everything about his profile points to him being even better in that sphere, especially with 3m still to try. Considering he's already achieved plenty over hurdles, that makes him a very exciting proposition, whether he starts out in novice handicaps (a lenient-looking mark of 130 will surely tempt connections) or level-weights company. If all goes well, it's not totally fanciful to suggest he could emulate some past greats who've carried the famous emerald green, yellow and white silks. Marown is from the family of mudlark Cannington Brook, and his three runs to date have all been on heavy going. Like that relative, he promises to stay very well. ***Nicky Richards***

Conclusion: ***Unbeaten in a bumper and two novice hurdles, but every inch a staying chaser and rates a very smart prospect for that discipline, this season and beyond***

McFabulous (Ire) h142p

6 b.g. Milan – Rossavon (Ire) (Beneficial)
2019/20 h16s² h15.7v⁴ h20.6d* h21d* Mar 14

The EBF Novices' Handicap Hurdle Final is invariably one of the best handicaps of its type run all season and always a rich source of promising horses for the following campaign. The 2020 edition, staged at Kempton a week later than usual after waterlogging claimed its regular spot in the calendar on Imperial Cup day at Sandown, was no different, and the winner McFabulous is as good a prospect as we've seen in the race for many a season.

An inclusion in last season's *Fifty* after an impressive bumper career, McFabulous got off to a shaky start over hurdles, getting turned over at 30/100 on his first try and finishing last of four next time, but he figured things out once upped in trip after Christmas, winning a small-field novice at Market Rasen prior to that EBF Final success. He did everything right at Kempton in the EBF Final, always going strongly and impressing with a slick round of jumping, and the way he came clear in the straight to defy a BHA mark of 132 was evidence of a horse with graded-race potential. Indeed, after the race Paul Nicholls said 'he could be a Stayers' Hurdle horse one day'. That suggests sticking to timber will be the plan for 2020/21, and McFabulous certainly has potential for more improvement in that sphere, but as a half-brother to the top-class chaser Waiting

McFabulous developed into a useful hurdler in the second half of last season

Patiently with the physique and demeanour to jump fences, for our money he'll be even more interesting if sent novice chasing. ***Paul Nicholls***

Conclusion: *Delivered on bumper promise when routing a field of unexposed rivals in the EBF Final in the spring and has the potential to prove very smart whether campaigned over hurdles or fences*

Mossy Fen (Ire) h133

5 b.g. Milan – Inch Native (IRE) (Supreme Leader)
2019/20 h23s* h20s* h24s^4 h21s* h21s^5 Mar 11

Mossy Fen was purchased for £60,000 after winning his only completed start in an Irish point in 2019, and it looks like money well spent based on what he achieved under Rules last season. A strong, rangy gelding, Mossy Fen is very much the type to make his mark when sent chasing, but he still managed to show useful form over hurdles, winning three times, notably the Grade 2 Leamington Novices' Hurdle at Warwick. He deserved extra credit on that occasion, too, as he still looked raw and barely found the 21f trip enough of a test, but he responded well under pressure to lead close home. It was interesting that connections decided to run him in the Ballymore Novices' Hurdle at Cheltenham on his final start as his run style suggested he would be much better suited by the three-mile trip of the Albert Bartlett at the Festival, but he ran about as well as could have been expected over a trip short of his optimum, finishing fifth. He can raise his game to another level when facing a suitable test of stamina over fences, and he is a smashing prospect. ***Nigel Twiston-Davies***

Conclusion: *Mossy Fen has all the attributes to develop into a smart novice chaser in 2020/21, plenty to like about him physically, and his experience in points is sure to stand him in good stead*

Percy Pops h104p

6 ch.g. Getaway (Ger) – Popsie Hall (Saddlers' Hall (Ire))

2019/20 b16s^{6} h16.8s h16.5s h19s^{3} h18.5v^{5} Feb 21

The all-action rides—think Johnson on Anzum or McCoy on Wichita Lineman—get the plaudits, but there's another type of great ride, when a jockey gets everything from a horse without resorting to the most obvious forms of persuasion. A classic of the genre is Denis O'Regan's effort on Giles Cross in the 2012 Grand National Trial at Haydock, when he worked magic holding together a horse who was on the verge of curling up and just resisted a strong finish from no less a rival than Neptune Collonges. That gruelling race bottomed Giles Cross—he never finished again—but the colours he carried have been back in action aboard Percy Pops, and we think he's one to follow in 2020/21.

Percy Pops is actually out of a full sister to Giles Cross, but on early evidence he's a different type to that fine long-distance chaser, having taken a strong hold in a hood in each of his starts to date. That goes some way to explaining why he's been dropped right out every time, but there's little doubt those tactics haven't seen him to good effect. In spite of that, Percy Pops has managed to show a fair bit of ability, notably when third at Taunton in January, and once he goes handicapping we reckon there'll be more than enough improvement in him to defy a BHA mark of 116, with a quick switch to a novice handicap chase perhaps an option given his breeding. ***Neil Mulholland***

Conclusion: *Merely laying foundations in four runs over hurdles last season and looks the type to leave those efforts well behind once handicapping, quite possibly over fences*

Pipesmoker (Fr) h125p

5 b.g. Authorized (Ire) – Pisa (Ger) (Sholokhov (Ire))

2019/20 b15.8d^{2} h16.8s^{3} h19.3v^{2} Feb 15

There's a common school of thought that suggests the best way to ensure a horse starts life in handicaps from a lenient mark is to try and mask its true level of ability in the early part of its career, often by running at lower-grade tracks against lesser opposition and attempting to disguise the real level of superiority. Such a policy does work from time to time, but it's interesting to note that the Henderson-trained Epatante, Champ, Might Bite, William Henry and Sign of A Victory all appeared at either Cheltenham, Ascot or Newbury (in some cases on more than one occasion) prior to making their first appearance in a handicap hurdle. And all made a winning start.

Hopefully, that'll be the case for Pipesmoker, too. He has been set tough tasks for both starts over hurdles so far, but finished a promising third behind stable-companion Chantry House in a novice at Cheltenham first time up before coming up against Sporting John in a similar event at Ascot a couple of months later. On both occasions Pipesmoker shaped like more of a staying type, which is rather at odds with his Flat-based pedigree, but it does mean that he remains with considerable potential. An opening BHA mark of 137 demands improvement but there's a good chance it could be on the lenient side given the quality of horses he's come up against (and got near to), no surprise if he's able to progress into something better than a handicapper in time, too. ***Nicky Henderson***

Conclusion: *Winning a maiden or novice will be a formality for Pipesmoker before he moves into handicaps and, as a slow-maturing type, he's just the sort that'll progress into something useful or better at 2½m+, no surprise if his first handicap appearance is in the race won by Champ at Newbury a few seasons back, The Cashel Man also successful for the yard in 2019*

Rath An Iuir (Ire) h120

7 b.g. Flemensfirth (USA) – Amathea (Fr) (Exit To Nowhere (USA))

2019/20 h20.5v⁴ h22v* h24.4s² h22v² Mar 14

The 2019/2020 season is another that Rose Dobbin would have been glad to see the back of, further issues after a troublesome previous campaign including a spell from mid-January in which she sent out no runners at all for a month. Indeed, a total of 17 winners from the past two seasons combined is still some way short of the 25 amassed in a productive 2017/18. One horse who could well help see the yard fare better in 2020/21 is the lightly raced and progressive Rath An Iuir.

Sold for six figures after getting off the mark on his third start in Irish points, Rath An Iuir was forced to miss a couple of years before making his debut over hurdles for current connections, scoring at Newcastle on his second start. He proved his stamina for 3m when second on his handicap debut next time before improving further in filling the same spot back at Newcastle shortly before the premature end to the season.

That promising first season under Rules really ought to be built upon now that his attentions will surely be turned to chasing—he impressed with his athleticism over hurdles and very much strikes as the type to take well to fences. The best of his dam's progeny so far is My Hometown, a fairly useful cross-country performer for Enda Bolger, and stamina looks a major asset of Rath An Iuir's too, so it's easy to see him doing well novice chasing over 3m+ in the North. ***Rose Dobbin***

Conclusion: *Steadily progressive in four starts over hurdles and type to do better with attentions turned to chasing, particularly as his stamina is drawn out*

Remastered h131

7 ch.g. Network (Ger) – Cathodine Cayras (Fr) (Martaline)
2019/20 h19.5s h21v5 h23.6v2 h23.4vpu h24.4v3 h19.9v3 Mar 14

'Remastering' refers to the process of improving the quality of a sound or image, and in the case of the David Pipe-trained Remastered we think this particular model could be improved plenty by a switch to chasing.

Remastered was always likely to need some time given how strapping a specimen he is, which makes his performance in running to a Timeform rating of 102 when winning a Chepstow bumper on his debut for current connections in February 2018 all the more noteworthy. A promising first season over hurdles, albeit one in which he was restricted to just three runs, wasn't really built upon in 2019/20, though he did run well back at Chepstow in early-December behind the subsequent Welsh National winner Potters Corner (other future winners behind, too), and he strung solid efforts together on his final two starts.

The extra time he was afforded over hurdles to mature should be rewarded now that he'll surely be tackling fences this season. By Network (the sire of Sprinter Sacre and Delta Work) out of a fairly useful French chase winner, herself by Martaline (the sire of Dynaste, the best chaser Pipe has trained), everything points to Remastered being a much better horse over the larger obstacles. He tended to lack a gear change over hurdles but the different dynamic of chasing, together with another summer on his back to help him fill his giant frame, should see him start to live up to his potential this season. Given his ability to plough through deep ground and his apparent suitability to Chepstow, Remastered could well be a Welsh National horse of the future and connections will no doubt be eyeing up a valuable staying handicap or two along the way. ***David Pipe***

Conclusion: *Everything suggests he should be much better over fences this season and is very much one to look out for in staying handicaps*

Rock On Rocco (Ire) h119

6 b.g. Shirocco (Ger) – Katalina (Hernando (Fr))
2019/20 b16d h20.3vpu h16.6d3 h15.8v* Feb 20

Some of the higher profile Roger Brookhouse-owned/Tom George-trained hurdlers haven't quite made the expected transition to chasing over the past couple of seasons, both Black Op and Summerville Boy returning to hurdles after two starts over fences. Rock on Rocco was nowhere near as high profile a hurdler as that pair, but there are firm hopes that he can make a smoother switch to the larger obstacles this season.

Having shown fair form in a couple of bumpers, Rock on Rocco flopped on his hurdling debut but progressed with both subsequent starts, placed behind Gaelik Coast at

Doncaster before winning cosily at Huntingdon, on both occasions looking a generally fluent, athletic jumper who has all the hallmarks of a much better chaser (as many by Shirocco are). Indeed, he may well progress considerably beyond an opening BHA mark of 117—which looks lenient in any case on his hurdles form—if pitched into a novice handicap chase straight away, though such is his trajectory that he'd make a fair bit of appeal from that mark if connections opt to stick over timber for the time being, too. Either way, after just five starts under Rules he's a horse that should have plenty more to offer and one that punters should be rewarded in following this season. ***Tom George***

Conclusion: *Very much went the right way in three starts over hurdles and looks well up to making his mark in handicaps if sticking to hurdling or, more likely, sent chasing*

Saint Sonnet (Fr) c142p

5 b.g. Saint des Saints (Fr) – Leprechaun Lady (Fr) (Irish Wells (Fr))
2019/20 c17.9g* h17.9s* h17.9s5 h19.4s6 h17.9v3 c19.2s* c19.8s Mar 12

Thrown into the deep end in the Golden Miller at Cheltenham on just his third start over fences (and just his second in Britain), Saint Sonnet coped better than might have been expected, promising more than the end result for a long way in fact. Indeed, the way he worked his way into contention down the hill, getting onto the heels of the leaders going pretty well turning for home, suggests he's a horse with a good bit more to offer yet, that he couldn't sustain his challenge perfectly understandable given the quality of the race combined with him having made quite a bad mistake in the back straight just as the race was starting to heat up.

It might only have been a small-field Catterick novice that Saint Sonnet had won the time before, but both the second and third won handicaps on the same card at Kelso the week after Cheltenham, and Saint Sonnet retains a lot of potential heading into his second season over fences and his first full one in Britain. A listed-winning four-year-old hurdler in France, both his physique and pedigree—his dam is a half-sister to the likes of Terrefort (dual Grade-1 winning novice chaser) and Vino Griego (also much better known as a chaser)—strongly suggest he'll prove a good bit better over fences than hurdles and he's still a young horse, too. An obvious first port of call this season is the BetVictor Gold Cup, a race in which Nicholls has a good recent record with French-bred youngsters, both Al Ferof and Caid du Berlais (as a five-year-old, in these colours) winning it in its former guise on their handicap debuts, and by our reckoning Saint Sonnet has the scope to make an impact in a race such as that from a BHA mark of 147. ***Paul Nicholls***

Conclusion: *Shaped promisingly faced with a very stiff task at Cheltenham and retains plenty of potential heading into his second season over fences, a big handicap likely to be on the agenda*

Schiehallion Munro c140

7 ch.g. Schiaparelli (Ger) – Mrs Fawlty (Kayf Tara)
2019/20 c19.2d* c19.1s^{2} c16.3s* c19.2d* Jan 22

2019/20 was a landmark season for Middleham trainer Micky Hammond. As well as winning his first Grade 1 courtesy of Cornerstone Lad in the Fighting Fifth, he also sent out his 1,000th winner. Hammond—who once raised money for charity by wearing shorts non-stop between November and March, including to race meetings, the doctor, and even a funeral!—can rightly be proud of that achievement considering he's mostly dealt with low-graders over the years, but Cornerstone Lad shows he's well capable with a good horse, and the likeable Schiehallion Munro could be the latest to ensure the stable is a presence on some of racing's bigger days.

Schiehallion Munro did well over hurdles in 2018/19, winning two novices, but his enthusiastic demeanour always pointed to him making a better chaser, and so it proved last season, when some accurate jumping saw him win three of his four starts. Each one of those came in smallish fields up North, but the form actually stacks up very well, twice beating next-time winners, while he was most impressive when landing a novice handicap at Catterick on his final outing, virtually hard held at the line in what was a well-contested race for the track. A 9 lb rise means Schiehallion Munro will start the new season from a mark of 140, which won't be a problem based on how he won at Catterick, and there are plenty of handicap chases up North for a horse in that bracket—his progressive profile will count for plenty. A keen-goer, he's effective from 2m to 2½m. ***Micky Hammond***

Conclusion: *Yet to run a bad race in his career and made a smooth transition to chasing last term; jumps well and very much the type to do well in Northern handicap chases at up to 2½m*

Shishkin (Ire) h159p

6 b.g. Sholokhov (Ire) – Labarynth (Ire) (Exit To Nowhere (USA))
2019/20 h16.3d^{F} h16.3s* h19.6s* h16.4s* Mar 10

'Paul—I've been lucky all my life, don't worry and I hope you ride many more winners for me' were reportedly the words offered by owner Joe Donnelly to Paul Townend the morning after the rider had bizarrely taken the wrong course in the closing stages of the Champion Novice Chase at the 2018 Punchestown Festival. The horse in question was, of course, Al Boum Photo, and Donnelly and Townend's fortunes did indeed turn around quite significantly so far as that one was concerned, the horse winning the next two renewals of the Gold Cup. The upbeat message to Townend was far more than post-race bluster—by all accounts Donnelly has found success in pretty much everything he's turned his hand to, most notably bookmaking and modern art collecting, but even by his standards going within a nose of winning three races at the Cheltenham Festival having only had runners in four was quite astonishing.

Shishkin was Donnelly's first horse with Nicky Henderson and, incidentally, is named after a Russian artist as opposed to the way Sean Connery pronounces the 2019 Phoenix Stakes winner Siskin. He'd looked something out of the ordinary from the start, winning a bumper at Kempton the day after Al Boum Photo won his first Gold Cup. He was installed as ante-post favourite for the Supreme soon after displaying an ultra-impressive turn of foot to win a novice hurdle at Newbury in January (he'd fallen early in a similar race at the track in December) but, with punters looking elsewhere for value on the day, ended up drifting markedly in the betting before the Festival curtain-raiser. Shishkin's SP—nearly 10/1 on the Betfair Exchange—looks particularly generous in hindsight given he had to overcome two significant pieces of interference on the way round, needing to show plenty of determination and stamina to overhaul Abacadabras on the run-in. Shishkin seems to have it all, including the physique/background for fences (point winner), and is probably the most exciting novice chasing prospect this side of the Irish sea, reportedly set to stick to two miles according to his trainer. ***Nicky Henderson***

Shishkin (right) and Abacadabras jump the last together in the Supreme

Conclusion: *Showed stamina and guts to go with his raw speed and ability when overcoming plenty of trouble in the Supreme and has all the qualities to believe he can go to the very top as a chaser*

Sizable Sam **b98**

5 ch.g. Black Sam Bellamy (Ire) – Halo Flora (Alflora (Ire))
2019/20 b15.3s² b16s* Feb 8

There's little doubt that less emphasis is placed on correct grammar and spelling than used to be the case. To such an extent that the Apostrophe Protection Society announced in November 2019 that 'ignorance and laziness' had won and that the society was to be shut down. The news story was picked up by many outlets, however, including The Guardian, generating such interest that the amount of traffic heading for the website exceeded the available bandwidth and resulted in the website being temporarily withdrawn for a completely different reason.

There have been many examples of hard-to-understand apostrophe use in horse names over the years, probably the highest profile being Big Buck's, the four-time Stayers' Hurdle winner, and even more instances of spelling making little sense. The connections of Sizable Sam doubtless have an explanation as to why the 'e' was omitted, but it's safe to assume that the omission will cause the name to be misspelled by plenty of journalists in the coming years. Hopefully, it'll be a name that crops up a lot in tipping columns and preview articles in 2020/21, the promise Sizable Sam showed in a couple of bumpers last season suggesting he's got a fine long-term future. He certainly displayed a good attitude on both starts, rallying when edged out in a large field at Wincanton on debut before again responding well to pressure when going one better at Warwick three months later, longer distances sure to suit when he goes hurdling. ***Jeremy Scott***

Conclusion: *His long-term future almost certainly lies as a chaser given his physique, but Sizable Sam seems sure to pick up a few races over hurdles first, his yard a dab hand at getting the most out of the talent at their disposal*

Southfield Harvest **h123p**

6 b.g. Kayf Tara – Chamoss Royale (Fr) (Garde Royale)
2019/20 h21.4s² h23.8v* Feb 19

Chamoss Royale was a useful performer over hurdles and fences for Paul Nicholls in the mid-noughties, and she's been at least as productive in her second career as a broodmare. Of her six foals to have raced—each one having the Southfield prefix—

three have proved smart, and if Southfield Harvest progresses as we think, that number will soon be four.

Southfield Harvest ran twice in bumpers in spring 2019, winning second time out at Chepstow at the main expense of Stolen Silver, who won a Grade 2 novice hurdle last season. We didn't see him again until January 2020, when he finished an encouraging second on his hurdling debut in a novice at Wincanton. That race was a steadily-run affair over 21f, and Southfield Harvest seemed to find it barely enough of a test, no surprise given the stamina in his pedigree. A step up to just short of 3m for his second go over hurdles at Ludlow seemed sure to suit, but it was another slowly-run race and, in the event, Southfield Harvest did very well to catch next-time winner Muckamore on the flat after that one had got first run.

The upshot is a horse who hasn't yet been able to show the full extent of his stamina or ability, and when he gets a proper test he can prove a mark of 127 totally inadequate. Sticking to hurdles will be an option but, given his breeding—two of his relatives won Grade 2 novice chases—a quick switch to fences will more than likely be the plan for Southfield Harvest. ***Paul Nicholls***

Conclusion: *From a good staying family and overcame the run of the race to make it second time lucky over hurdles; has plenty of scope for further improvement and can prove an opening mark of 127 lenient*

St Barts (Ire) h126p

6 b.g. High Chaparral (Ire) – Lindeman (Ire) (Presenting)
2019/20 h19.3s⁶ h19.9v* h21.4s³ h23.5v* Feb 15

Every now and then a horse gets a BHA mark that leaves people mystified. Usually, it's when a horse goes handicapping from a mark that bears no relation to its lack of achievements in novice hurdles, but sometimes (and to be fair not all that often!) the BHA Handicapper gets it badly wrong the other way. St Barts was one such example from last season and, though the assessor has attempted to take corrective action in the meantime, we think St Barts can remain ahead of his mark for a while yet.

After an encouraging mid-field finish in a maiden at Ascot on his Rules debut in November, St Barts was a wide-margin winner of a similar race at Uttoxeter the following month, ahead of a next-time winner. He managed only third under a penalty at Wincanton next time, but that was a strong race (fellow *Fifty* member Southfield Harvest was second), and a steady gallop didn't suit a stoutly-bred one who already looked in need of 3m. The Uttoxeter form might easily have justified a mark in the mid or high-120s—horses who have achieved less regularly get similar—but St Barts was given 118 and it's a measure of that perceived leniency that he went off 2/1 in a 15-runner race on his handicap debut at Ascot. As expected, St Barts relished the longer trip that day, and with crack claimer Ben Jones on board he never gave his backers much cause for concern.

A 7 lb rise for Ascot looks on the lenient side again and, as an unexposed horse whose stamina hasn't yet been fully tested, St Barts should continue to progress. His Derby-winning sire has produced some good chasers, notably Altior, and a switch to fences could also be an option for St Barts, who won a British point in March 2019. ***Philip Hobbs***

Conclusion: *Benefited from generosity from the assessor when scoring on handicap debut but going the right way in general and looks a useful stayer in the making, with chasing an option*

Tamaroc du Mathan (Fr) h130

5 b.g. Poliglote – Thisbee du Mathan (Fr) (Turgeon (USA))
2019/20 h15.7s[2] h15.7v h16.3g[5] h21d Mar 14

Despite his star horse Cyrname failing to meet expectations when sent off favourite for the King George, 2019/20 was another successful season for owner Johnny de la Hey, whose runners broke the £300,000 barrier in prize money for the third successive term. That's quite an impressive figure considering only seven of his horses won races and is an indication of the quality of his string, who are sourced from France for undisclosed amounts (impressive Adonis winner Solo is rumoured to have cost something in the region of £750,000).

One of those seven winners was Pic d'Orhy, who'd arrived in Britain from Francois Nicolle's yard with some strong form to his name—second in a Grade 1—and a lofty reputation, prominent in the ante-post market for the Triumph before he'd even made the track for Paul Nicholls. He finally put it all together in the Betfair Hurdle last season but wasn't the only De la Hey/Nicholls horse to put up an improved effort in the race, Tamaroc du Mathan running on quite takingly for fifth. He was unable to build on that effort next time at Kempton, racing too keenly up in trip, but, as with Pic d'Orhy and so many other Nicholls horses, it seems only a matter of time before everything clicks into place. Kempton was only his fifth start and Tamaroc du Mathan is likely to stay 2½m once learning to settle down. ***Paul Nicholls***

Conclusion: *Still a work in progress but shaped promisingly in the Betfair Hurdle and seems sure to be winning races soon for top connections*

The Big Breakaway (Ire) h137p

5 ch.g. Getaway (Ger) – Princess Mairead (Ire) (Blueprint (Ire))
2019/20 h19.5s* h20.5d* h21s^4 Mar 11

When it comes to buying horses there are clearly no half measures for owners Eric Jones, Geoff Nicholas and John Romans. Between them, they spent well over half a million pounds on their first two recruits, but in the current climate—where a regressive Don Poli is apparently worth £170,000—it's hard to say their strategy isn't paying off. Slate House, the group's first buy, finally realised his potential as a chaser during 2019/20, winning the Grade 1 Kauto Star at Kempton after an agonising late fall in the BetVictor Gold Cup, while The Big Breakaway made a highly promising start to his hurdling career, winning at Chepstow and Newbury before posting a respectable fourth in the Ballymore at Cheltenham in March.

That last effort came during a particularly frustrating week for The Big Breakaway's trainer Colin Tizzard and is probably worth marking up as a result, even if he was never dangerous and beaten nearly 15 lengths by Envoi Allen. Despite making half the number of starts The Big Breakaway is rated just 1 lb lower than Slate House was after his novice hurdling campaign and looks set to make at least as good a chaser as that one (another rangy, chasing type), hopefully hitting the ground running over fences in 2020/21. ***Colin Tizzard***

Conclusion: *Good fourth in Ballymore during a notably quiet week for yard and seems sure to improve for the switch to fences given his physique and background*

The Glancing Queen (Ire) b107

6 b.m. Jeremy (USA) – Glancing (Ire) (Kayf Tara)
2019/20 b16.4s Mar 11

The 2019 Champion Bumper might have attracted the smallest field in its history, but it still looked a strong race beforehand and subsequent events have proved it most certainly was. The first four home were Envoi Allen, Blue Sari, Thyme Hill and Abacadabras, three of whom are now rated at least 149 over hurdles by Timeform. Fifth that day was The Glancing Queen, and she was a bit better than the result, too, having been stuck in traffic approaching the straight. Three weeks later she won the Grade 2 bumper for mares at the Grand National meeting, again travelling notably strongly for a long way before knuckling down well when pressured, the placed horses that day (Minella Melody and Daylight Katie) having gone on to show themselves promising novice hurdlers the following season. The Glancing Queen herself didn't manage to make it over hurdles last season, her return to the track delayed by sore shins and a splint, but she did have another crack at the Champion Bumper, shaping a lot better than eighth of 23 behind Ferny Hollow might suggest, tiring after making

The Glancing Queen (left) can put together a sequence over hurdles

a big move out wide running down the hill. That run strongly suggested that the absence hadn't had a detrimental effect on The Glancing Queen, and, as the winner of her only start in points, it's hard to believe she won't be effective over a fair bit further than two miles when the time comes. ***Alan King***

Conclusion: *The jumps programme caters for mares so much better than used to be the case that it's surely a question of 'how many' when The Glancing Queen makes her delayed start over hurdles, highly likely she'll run up a sequence before being upped in grade in the second half of the season and maybe the one to break Willie Mullins' stranglehold on the Dawn Run*

The Mulcair (Ire) h121

6 b.g. Flemensfirth (USA) – Black Lassie (Ire) (Dr Massini (Ire))

2019/20 h24v* h24s^pu Dec 14

Dan Skelton has few peers in Britain when it comes to target training, so much so that he and Willie Mullins have had the County Hurdle—one of the most fiercely-competitive handicap hurdle races in the calendar—between themselves since 2015. Skelton's most recent County winner was Ch'tibello in 2019, the same season in which he broke through the 200-winner barrier, but much like a horse having its next run after a big target, Skelton failed to back up that huge effort in the most recent season, dropping to 119 winners.

The Skelton yard was still operating at a respectable 16% strike rate in 2019/20 but it'll be no surprise at all if he's back up to around 20% this season, and one horse who seems sure to pick up a couple of races at the very least is The Mulcair, who made a winning Rules debut at Southwell over hurdles in 2019. At the time, handing an 11-length beating to Jepeck in receipt of weight wasn't especially noteworthy, for all that The Mulcair travelled and jumped well, but the form looks a lot better in hindsight, Jepeck winning his next two starts, including back over fences in the Veterans' Final at Sandown in January. The Mulcair himself failed to deal with a marked step up in grade at Cheltenham a month later, but that's not to say he won't develop into a graded performer in time as a chaser, a strapping winning Irish pointer from the family of Imperial Commander. ***Dan Skelton***

Conclusion: ***Not seen since disappointing in a Grade 2 at Cheltenham but made pleasing winning hurdles debut prior to that and, every inch a chaser on looks, is expected to make a quick—and successful—switch to fences this term***

Ben Fearnley, Racing Analyst (The Mulcair): *"As many of the Timeform Editorial department will attest – looks aren't everything in life. However, when it comes to horses they can certainly get you a long way and it was hard not to be taken by The Mulcair on debut, towering over and outjumping Jepeck when handing him an emphatic beating at Southwell. The Mulcair's disappointing effort up in grade at Cheltenham next time is easy to forgive and he seems sure to win a couple of novice chases at the very least this season."*

Third Time Lucki (Ire) b114

5 br.g. Arcadio (Ger) – Definite Valley (Ire) (Definite Article)
2019/20 b15.7s3 b16.6s* b15.8s* b16.4s4 Mar 11

It was second time lucky for Third Time Lucki in his bumper campaign as, after arguably shaping best in a large-field affair at Ascot on debut, he looked a smart prospect when justifying favouritism in a lesser event at Market Rasen without coming off the bridle. The way he defied a penalty from a Henderson newcomer at Huntingdon next time confirmed that he was one of the best British-trained bumper horses, and he proved that by faring best of the home contingent in the Champion Bumper on his final outing. Third Time Lucki was beaten six lengths into fourth by Ferny Hollow at the Festival, suited by a patient ride in a well-run race and seeing things out strongly having been unable to quicken when initially asked. It looked a strong renewal, too, and Ferny Hollow put up one of the best winning performances in recent years. Unsurprisingly, plenty took the eye physically, too, and whilst Third Time Lucki wasn't one of the more prepossessing types with chasing in mind (he was seemingly outstayed when runner-up on his sole start in points), he has so much speed that he'll need to jump with only a degree of accuracy to ensure his novice hurdling campaign is a fruitful one. ***Dan Skelton***

Conclusion: *It's no mean feat to get in amongst the Irish-trained horses in the Champion Bumper—Thyme Hill was the only one from Britain to manage it in the 2019 renewal—and Third Time Lucki deserved considerable credit for making the frame, his speed likely to take him a long way in the novice hurdling ranks in 2020/21*

Timberman (Ire) 119P

5 b.g. Califet (Fr) – Millrock Lady (Ire) (Court Cave (Ire))
2019/20 b16.3g^2 h16v^5 Dec 7

Last season was the first since 1994/95 when the Champion Jockey wasn't named either McCoy or Johnson, Brian Hughes having 19 winners in hand over defending champion Johnson by the time proceedings ended abruptly in mid-March. There's been a similar lack of variety when it comes to champion trainer, Martin Pipe, Paul Nicholls and Nicky Henderson having shared the last 25 titles, 2019/20 seeing Henderson land his sixth championship 34 years on from the first. Between them, Hughes and Henderson had 259 winners last season, but they teamed up just once, when Timberman made his hurdling debut in a 2m novice at Sandown in December.

Sent off 7/2 second favourite at Sandown having finished an encouraging second in a Newbury bumper the previous month, Timberman could only manage fifth, 17 lengths behind the winner Fiddlerontheroof, but he was better than those bare facts suggest, travelling as well as any but not lasting out having jumped two out in second. That was a strong race, five of the first six having won since, and it would surely have been all six had we seen Timberman out again. His absence perhaps points to a problem, but it may not be a bad thing for his long-term development—he's only a five-year-old and is unfurnished at present. That he's still a novice means Timberman will have a wealth of options open to him, and it'd be a surprise if he isn't up to winning a couple of regulation novices at the very least, with major improvement on the cards. He hasn't looked short of pace on either start so far, but there's enough stamina on the dam's side of his pedigree to suggest he'll have no problem with further than 2m. ***Nicky Henderson***

Conclusion: *Major promise in a hot race on his sole outing over hurdles last winter and open to significant improvement with that under his belt*

Topofthegame c162p

8 ch.g Flemensfirth (USA) – Derry Vale (Ire) (Mister Lord (USA))
2018/19 c19.2s^{2} c24g^{2} c24.4s* c25d^{2} Apr 5

In the interests of value for money we try to avoid including too many of the same entrants in successive *Fifty* lists, though in some cases—as with Highland Hunter, Imperial Aura and McFabulous this year—certain horses are simply too interesting to ignore even if they have featured in a previous edition. Topofthegame must be the first ever to appear in three editions of *Horses to Follow*. His original inclusion—in 2017/18—was with a view to him going chasing and he ended up having just one start in that sphere that season (fell on debut at Newbury).

Indeed, patience has very much been the name of the game with Topofthegame, his 2019/20 campaign over through injury before it even had a chance to begin, though connections would surely have been quietly pleased to see how his form from the previous season worked out. His runs at the Cheltenham and Aintree Festivals tie him in closely with last season's Gold Cup second (Santini, now rated 170), third (Lostintranslation, 168) and fifth (Delta Work, 168) and it'd come as something of a surprise if Topofthegame didn't develop into a 170+ horse himself eventually, particularly as he still looked quite raw at times that season, rather worried out of

Topofthegame (right) is expected to make up for lost time this season

it after hitting the front in the Kauto Star at Kempton. Reportedly the tallest horse Paul Nicholls has ever trained, his extended break from the racecourse could end up proving a blessing in disguise, allowing him to develop even further physically, and he's expected to take high rank amongst the very best staying chasers this season, the Ladbrokes Trophy at Newbury looking a suitable starting point. ***Paul Nicholls***

Conclusion: *Bang there with the likes of Santini, Lostintranslation and Delta Work based on novice form and has the potential to make up into a strong Gold Cup contender*

Wasdell Dundalk (Fr) h107p

5 ch.g. Spirit One (Fr) – Linda Queen (Fr) (Linda's Lad)

2019/20 b15.8d4 b17.1s h16.5d4 h16.2v6 h15.5v5 :: 2020/21 h17.7m4 Aug 18

Martin Tedham has owned horses for a while – think the likes of Michael Flips and Bible Lord trained by Andy Turnell – but, after a spell out of the sport due to a major health scare, Martin is back with a renewed vigour and kitty judged on the £440,000 he splashed out on Papa Tango Charly at the 2019 Aintree sale, while he's also now the sponsor of Jonjo O'Neill's Jackdaws Castle yard. Tedham's spending power isn't matched by any originality in the naming department, however, given that over the past couple of seasons horses running in his colours include Tedham (a useful handicap hurdler), Wasdell (the name of the pharmaceutical packaging company he runs – the equine version performing nowhere near as successfully as the business) and The French Horse (not hard to guess what suffix follows that horse's name). A variation on a theme of one of the above is Wasdell Dundalk (the location of one of the company's facilities), and by our reckoning he's a name to follow this season.

A close fourth at Taunton on his hurdling debut, Wasdell Dundalk wasn't at all knocked about on his next couple of runs, all three starts coming in the space of a month before the turn of the year. He was on the sidelines for eight months subsequently and duly looked rusty when fourth on his handicap debut at Fontwell in August, coming off the bridle a long way out before doing his best work at the finish to be beaten only three and a quarter lengths. The way he shaped suggests he'll have even more to offer when stepping up to 2½m, also having the physical scope to suggest he'll go on improving, and a BHA mark of 111 is unlikely to prove beyond him on another day judged on his useful pedigree (his dam is closely related to the very smart chaser Hinterland). ***Jonjo O'Neill***

Conclusion: *Brought along with handicaps in mind over hurdles last season and really ought to be able to win races from a lowly mark in relation to his pedigree*

Young Bull (Ire) **h130p**

6 b.g. Yeats (Ire) – Pepsi Starlet (Ire) (Heavenly Manna)
2019/20 h19.7d³ h20v* h21.3v* h21.3v* h26v² Mar 8

Even though the season was cut short, 2019/20 was Harry Whittington's best by some margin, his 30 winners (from 160 runners) including a first Cheltenham Festival success—via Simply The Betts in the Plate—helping him to amass just under £500,000 in prize-money, nearly double his previous best. Three of Whittington's total victories last season came via the likeable Young Bull, who won a maiden at Ffos Las and a novice and handicap at Wetherby in November/December, responding well to pressure and shaping like a strong stayer on each occasion.

Despite the impression he'd created over 2½m, Young Bull failed to improve significantly on his first try over a long distance—at Warwick in early-March—but that was a strange race in which the winner Potters Hedger made most in a muddling contest, essentially given a far more efficient ride than Young Bull, and it's hard to believe he won't prove very well suited by that sort of trip in a more conventional contest. Runner-up on his sole start in Irish points, he'll make up into a staying chaser in future but would be able to win more races over hurdles at around 3m should connections wish to bide their time (Young Bull is still only six), a mark of 133 looking attractive considering his potential as a stayer. ***Harry Whittington***

Conclusion: *Tries hard and has untapped potential at 3m+, his defeat on sole start at that trip easy to forgive, his attitude and physique suggesting he'll be even better over fences*

LESS THAN £2.30 A DAY

Race Passes are the ultimate form guide, featuring ratings, all the Timeform Flags, In-Play Hints and symbols, live bookmakers prices - plus unlimited use of a 12-year form archive with Horse, Jockey and Trainer Searches. Subscriptions give you open access to Timeform data, starting from just £10 for 24 hours, to £75 for 28 days. Our best value subscription costs less than £2.30 a day though, when you sign-up by recurring payment.

RACE PASS Monthly

PayPal RECURRING PAYMENTS

Race Passes

Ratings. Flags. Form. In-Play.
Search any horse, any race, any time.

Why use Race Passes? What's more? visit bit.ly/TFRPGuide to explore our interactive guide. You'll bet better.

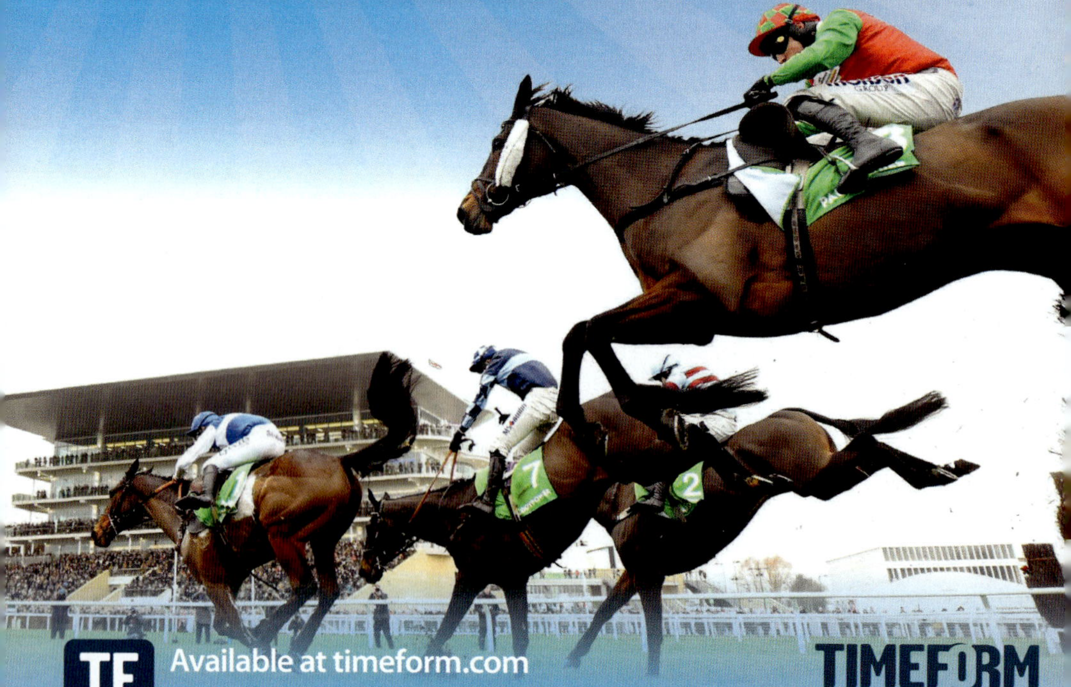

TF Available at timeform.com and to view on the App

TIMEFORM
PLAY SMARTER

SECTION 2

At The Acorn (Ire) h121p c131p

6.b.g Gold Well – Sister Trix (Ire) (Broken Hearted)
2019/20 c16s^{6} c21.2s c20v^{4} c17s^{6} c21.5v* c21s^{6} Feb 2

As of the end of 2019 there were over 3,000 horse names permanently protected by the International Federation of Horseracing Authorities. To have a name permanently protected usually means that a horse has achieved great things on the track or in the breeding shed, but it still must have been a shock to those who followed Mrs S. Harbour's maiden hurdler At The Acorn in the mid-90s to see him finally get his head in front in a Fairyhouse novice chase for Tony Martin 24 years later. In all seriousness, a name and an initial failure to win over hurdles are the only things that Tony Martin's €150,000 point-to-point graduate shares with his modest predecessor. Placed on both of his starts over the smaller obstacles in 2018/19, it took At The Acorn a couple of runs to find his feet over fences, but a promising effort over an inadequate trip in a red-hot handicap at Leopardstown over Christmas sparked a change in his fortunes and he made no mistake when returned to novice company/a more suitable trip at Fairyhouse 16 days later, beating subsequent dual winner The Long Mile by a very cosy two-and-a-half lengths, the pair well clear.

Though At The Acorn couldn't justify strong support on his next start—back at Leopardstown for a valuable handicap at the Dublin Racing Festival—he shaped sufficiently well in sixth, hampered on more than one occasion, notably so when closing at the last (usual two out). That may not have been the end to the season connections envisaged but it did at least highlight that At The Acorn is still well handicapped from a mark of 131 over fences and, with the prospect of even more to come from him, including back over hurdles, it will be a huge surprise if his trainer—so often referred to as a handicap expert—can't place him to advantage on more than one occasion in 2020/21. ***Tony Martin***

Conclusion: *Unexposed type who boasts some strong form and remains attractively handicapped over fences*

Bob Olinger (Ire) b107P

5 b.g. Sholokhov (Ire) – Zenaide (Ire) (Zaffaran (USA))
2019/20 b18v* Mar 7

With less than 20 large Ps doled out in bumpers since the beginning of 2013/14, and fewer than half that number getting a triple-figure rating to go alongside the symbol, Bob Olinger entered a select group when making a winning start under Rules at Gowran in March. As you'd expect, the vast majority of those handed the 'P' went on to pay their way and a couple have really lived up to their early billing, namely Grade

1 winners Royal Vacation and Champ, all of which bodes really well for the prospects of Bob Olinger in 2020/21.

Privately purchased following a facile win on his sole point-to-point start, Bob Olinger and fellow point winner/Rules debutant Coqolino dominated the betting at Gowran, the latter's form having already been boosted by one he brushed aside that day (Smurphy Enki recorded a rating of 106 when routing his rivals in a Wincanton bumper). The race itself was one-sided, though, Bob Olinger travelling strongly at the head of affairs and putting the race to bed in a matter of strides, having 10 lengths to spare over the aforementioned rival at the line.

Obviously, he didn't get to take his chance at any of the big spring meetings in Ireland, but it will be a big surprise if he doesn't make a splash when sent hurdling, especially as he is a half-brother to a couple who proved useful in that sphere and with a yard who can be counted on to have him well schooled. All in all, Bob Olinger rates a most exciting prospect and it would be no surprise were he to have graded races in his sights in 2020/21. ***Henry de Bromhead***

Conclusion: *Could hardly have been more impressive when making a winning bumper debut and looks sure to make his mark over hurdles*

Fakir (Fr) h135

5 b.g. Day Flight – Lazary (Fr) (Bobinski)

2019/20 h16v^{5} h20.2s h16v^{6} h16v* h19.5v^{ur} h20v* Feb 15

Like his father before him, 27-year-old Joseph O'Brien has already made a big impact on National Hunt racing and has a big team of jumpers to go to war with again. One of those with a slightly lower profile—but plenty of potential to make a big name for himself—is Fakir. Though he won the second of his two starts in bumpers in his native France (beating Fred, who won a couple of novice hurdles for Nicky Henderson last season), Fakir ended up taking a little time to get going in Ireland, beaten by over 10 lengths on his first three starts. However, with the very promising claimer Oakley Brown taking over in the saddle for the first time, he eventually made a breakthrough in a 2m novice at Limerick in late-December. After a mishap at Down Royal on his next start (unseated at the fifth) he improved another chunk to make a winning handicap debut at Gowran Park in February, coming from well off the pace to rout the opposition in a race that turned into a real slog. Given how strong he was at the finish that day, it seems safe to assume that Fakir will relish the step up to 3m in time, and the Irish handicapper could certainly have been harsher on him for his 11-length victory (raised 10 lb to 131). He has the potential to make into a smart staying hurdler this season. ***Joseph O'Brien***

Conclusion: *Impressed with strength of finish when winning final start of last season and seems sure to have even more to offer once upped to 3m, his handicap mark still looking attractive*

Ferny Hollow (Ire) b123

5 b.g. Westerner – Mirazur (Ire) (Good Thyne (USA))

2019/20 b16s^{2} b16s^{2} b16v* b16.4s* Mar 11

Victory in the Champion Bumper does not guarantee a successful career over jumps. A quick glance through the roll of honour will show that while a handful of winners went on to become household jumping names (Florida Pearl, Alexander Banquet, Cue Card) there have also been plenty who never really fulfilled their potential (Hairy Molly, Cork All Star, Liberman). 2019 winner Envoi Allen is already threatening to join the former group and comparisons can certainly be drawn between him and the most recent winner, Ferny Hollow. Both started their racing life in the care of Colin Bowe and won their only start in a point prior to being sold for big money to Cheveley Park Stud (Envoi Allen cost £400,000 and Ferny Hollow 'just' £300,000).

Unlike Envoi Allen, Ferny Hollow was beaten in his first two bumpers, though that was largely his own doing, pulling too hard on both occasions, and it wasn't a surprise

Ferny Hollow runs out a decisive winner of the Champion Bumper

that the fitting of a hood combined with a more patient ride had a very positive effect, winning hard held at Fairyhouse in February. Patrick Mullins, onboard Ferny Hollow for his first three starts, opted to ride the higher-rated favourite Appreciate It at Cheltenham and, with the Mullins team still in search of a first winner of the Festival, Ferny Hollow was sent off a relatively unconsidered 11/1 shot. Ridden patiently once again—by Paul Townend this time—Ferny Hollow came through stylishly to pick off his stable companion inside the final furlong, finding plenty for pressure despite being keen in the early stages. That finishing effort combined with his pointing background/ pedigree suggests that Ferny Hollow will be suited by 2½m in time—once he learns to settle down—but that's certainly not to say he lacks for speed, similar to Envoi Allen in that way, too. Hopefully Ferny Hollow will prove more Champagne Fever than Joe Cullen. ***Willie Mullins***

Conclusion: *Champion Bumper winner who is still far from the finished article and is obviously an excellent novice hurdling prospect this season, particularly with further than 2m in mind*

Minella Indo (Ire) c160p

7 b.g. Beat Hollow – Carrigeen Lily (Ire) (Supreme Leader)

2019/20 h24d* c20v² c24s* c24.4s² Mar 11

Minella Indo holds the distinction of being one of very few horses to shed a maiden tag over hurdles at the highest level (in the 2019 Albert Bartlett) and he was robbed of the chance to repeat that feat over fences due to a spell of unseasonably dry weather last December, a late scratch from the Neville Hotels Novice Chase at Leopardstown after finishing second to Laurina on chase debut at Gowran Park in November. The ground was much more to connections' liking at Navan in mid-January and Minella Indo duly justified short odds in a maiden chase. Though he wasn't flashy in winning, the form received a significant boost when the runner-up Captain CJ went on to win a Grade 2 at the same track on his next start. Even with that form working out, lining up in the RSA on the back of just two starts in maiden chases was hardly ideal for Minella Indo, the last horse to win the race with a similar preparation (having not even contested a graded chase) being Lord Noelie some 20 years earlier, and even that one had had the benefit of four previous chase starts. It therefore augurs extremely well for Minella Indo that, having got the better of a prolonged duel with old rival Allaho, he was only picked off very late on by Champ's freakish late rally. With his career under Rules still just eight races in, there is surely still plenty more to come from him, trips in excess of 3m—including that of the Gold Cup—likely to hold no fears for connections. ***Henry de Bromhead***

Minella Indo (left) and Allaho (right) go head-to-head in the RSA

Conclusion: *Coped notably well with the RSA considering his unorthodox preparation and is entitled to progress even further as a second-season chaser, a top-class prospect for 3m+*

Minella Melody (Ire) h133

6 b.m. Flemensfirth (USA) – Cottage Theatre (Ire) (King's Theatre (Ire)
2019/20 b16.3d^{3} h20v* h19.7v* h18s* h16.8s Mar 12

The most recent addition to the Cheltenham Festival roster, the Dawn Run, has proved to be something of a Willie Mullins benefit—like many other Grade 1 races—since its inception in 2016. Mullins has won all five renewals to date, including with Concertista in 2020, though, incidentally, the also-rans have arguably gone on to have more of an impact on the overall jumping scene compared to the winners. Verdana Blue, La Bague Au Roi and Epatante all failed to place in the race in recent seasons, and we're hoping that Minella Melody, a major disappointment in the most recent renewal, can bounce back as those mares did.

As a bumper mare Minella Melody was placed in graded races at both the Aintree and Punchestown Festivals and, given her background in points, always seemed likely to take high rank over jumps. She took to hurdling very well, winning her first three starts, the pick of which being the Grade 3 Solerina Hurdle at Fairyhouse in

January where, despite the drop back to 2¼m, she proved too strong for a field which included Colreevy, Dolcita and Yukon Lil. The fact that trio went on to finish second, fourth and fifth respectively in the Dawn Run merely underlines just how far below-par Minella Melody was at Cheltenham, and she still remains a bright jumping prospect, particularly if, as expected, she is sent chasing. A lengthy, rather unfurnished mare, she's just the type that her trainer will excel with over fences and she should get another crack at a Grade 1 in time. ***Henry de Bromhead***

Conclusion: *Cheltenham disappointment does little to dent her overall potential and she looks to have all the raw materials to make up into a smart chaser*

Off You Go (Ire) c132p

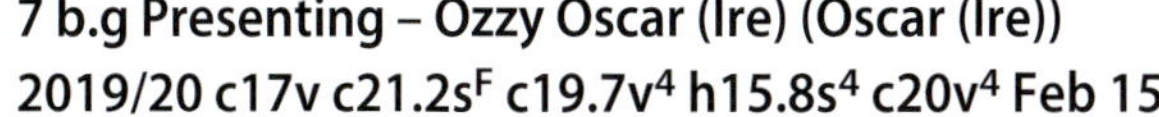

7 b.g Presenting – Ozzy Oscar (Ire) (Oscar (Ire))
2019/20 c17v c21.2s^{F} c19.7v^{4} h15.8s^{4} c20v^{4} Feb 15

On the face of it, a horse who has been beaten an average of 31 lengths in three completed starts over fences doesn't necessarily leap off the page as one to follow. However, one suspects that there'll be a fair bit more to come under the right circumstances, and Off You Go retains plenty of potential as a chaser.

A smart hurdler (two-time winner of the Ladbrokes Hurdle at Leopardstown), Off You Go was given a considerate introduction to chasing when failing to make an impact behind Fakir d'Oudairies and Melon at Navan but was in the process of showing markedly improved form when coming down at the last in another warm maiden (won by Carefully Selected) at Fairyhouse next time. Though he managed to make the frame in a similar event at Gowran in mid-February (his final start of the season), it's surely in handicaps where we'll see Off You Go realise his potential in 2020/21, his connections likely to have an eye on a premier handicap chase or two, his IHRB rating (138) looking attractive based on his hurdling exploits. ***Charles Byrnes***

Conclusion: *Gave every indication that he'll be capable of matching his smart hurdling form over fences when everything falls into place; potentially well treated on the pick of those efforts and one to watch out for in handicaps*

Queens Brook (Ire) b111

5 b.m. Shirocco (Ger) – Awesome Miracle (Ire) (Supreme Leader)
2019/20 b17v* b16.4s^{3} Mar 11

The colours of Noel and Valerie Moran were sported by a number of promising youngsters in 2019/20, Martin Pipe fifth The Bosses Oscar being the pick of the hurdlers—all based with Gordon Elliott—but several others laid positive foundations for the future, not least Champion Bumper third Queens Brook. The £160,000 connections parted with to secure Queens Brook—following a point win for Aidan Fitzgerald—was arguably vindicated straight away after she'd annihilated a 17-runner field at Gowran Park on bumper debut, leading early in the straight and pulling well clear (won by 21 lengths) on very testing ground.

Her run behind Ferny Hollow at Cheltenham the following month—where she pressed the leader on the home turn and was simply unable to quicken in the final furlong—ended her first season under Rules on an extremely positive note and, with the prospect of much more to come over hurdles, especially when faced with longer trips (bred to stay well and clearly possesses plenty of stamina based on the style of her win), she's a mare to follow in 2020/21. ***Gordon Elliott***

Conclusion: *Useful bumper performer who should take very high rank amongst her own sex in Ireland over the winter months, particularly with 2½m in mind*

Saint Roi (Fr) h150p

5 br.g. Coastal Path – Sainte Vigne (Fr) (Saint des Saints (Fr))

2019/20 h19.2s^5 h16s* h16.8d* Mar 13

When trying to find the winner of the Champion Hurdle it seems the best place to start is with horses owned by J. P. McManus. National Hunt racing's number-one patron has seen his green and gold silks carried to victory in the race no less than nine times, including in five of the last seven years. McManus looks to have another tight grip on the race this time around, too, with current champion Epatante hopefully joined by the returning Buveur d'Air, himself bidding to join a select group of three-time winners. However, it's not out of the question that a third contender could emerge in the form of Saint Roi.

Like plenty of other McManus horses Saint Roi began his racing career in France, purchased after a promising third in a listed juvenile contest at Auteuil (when trained by G. Cherel) in 2018. He failed to meet expectations (sent off at 1/3) on debut for Willie Mullins at Clonmel in December but proved an entirely different proposition at Tramore on New Year's Day, barely having to come off the bridle to readily dismiss a field which included subsequent dual winner Arcadian Sunrise. Despite being allotted a BHA rating of 137 on the back of that, Saint Roi was well backed for the County Hurdle at Cheltenham and made a complete mockery of that opening mark, running out a most comprehensive winner of what is traditionally one of the strongest handicaps of the entire year. Trying to put that performance into context isn't easy but it is worth pointing out that Saint Roi won from a very similar mark to two of Mullins' other previous winners of the race, Thousand Stars (134) and Wicklow Brave (138), both of whom went on to win Grade 1s. For further context, 137 is incidentally also the same mark that Epatante defied on her handicap debut/reappearance at Newbury in November and, considering Saint

Saint Roi (centre) justifies strong support in the County Hurdle

Roi is still just four runs into his hurdling career, it wouldn't be a huge shock to see the pair lining up against each other on the Tuesday of the Festival. ***Willie Mullins***

Conclusion: *Notably well backed to win the County and remains something of an unknown quantity after just four starts for Willie Mullins; could well develop into a Grade 1 hurdler*

The Big Getaway (Ire) h148p

6 b.g. Getaway (Ger) – Saddlers Dawn (Ire) (Saddlers' Hall (Ire))

2019/20 b16.2d^{2} b16.5s* h20.3d^{4} h19s* h21s^{3} Mar 11

You can certainly see where the 'Big' comes from in The Big Getaway's moniker—he's a gigantic point winner who is every bit a chaser on looks. With that in mind, it's to his credit that he's been able to achieve what he has in bumpers and over hurdles, registering wide-margin victories in both those divisions before lining up in the Ballymore at Cheltenham.

Though he was readily brushed aside at the business end of that race by the exceptional Envoi Allen, The Big Getaway arguably enhanced his reputation even further, travelling as strongly as any for a long way and boxing on well enough in the closing stages, nudging his rating up another stone in the process. For obvious reasons we didn't see The Big Getaway after Cheltenham but in truth there wasn't a whole lot more he could have done to impress us further over hurdles, the seeds of excitement for a novice chasing campaign already well and truly sown. Owner Joe Donnelly has quite a few horses to look forward to in 2020/21 and The Big Getaway is certainly one of them. ***Willie Mullins***

Conclusion: *Big, strong gelding who should build on his smart hurdling form significantly when sent chasing this term*

SECTION 3

TALKING TO THE TRAINERS

We asked a number of leading National Hunt trainers to pick out a chaser, hurdler and novice to follow for the coming season. Here's what they said...

Brian Ellison

British winners in 2019/20 (best seasonal tally)	**34 (48)**
* Impact Value in 2019/20	**2.04**
Percentage of rivals beaten in 2019/20	**61.14**
Timeform Run to Form % in 2019/20	**52.14**
Return at BSP in 2019/20	**+75.36**
Highest-rated horse in training	**Definitly Red** Timeform Rating c162

** Impact Value is expressed as a factor of a trainer's number of winners compared to those expected to occur by chance*

Chaser: Windsor Avenue (c145): "We've lots of nice ones, like Sam's Adventure and The King of May, but Windsor Avenue is an absolute tool at home. He was good on his first two starts over fences but was disappointing at Doncaster. We had him checked afterwards but nothing really came to light, so we sent him to Haydock where Brian (Hughes) said he just stopped underneath him. We had him checked again and they found that he was choking in his races, so he's been hobdayed [wind operation] and hopefully that'll sort him out. He'll be aimed at some nice staying handicaps this season."

Hurdler: Whiskey and Water (h111): "He's a horse I like, but he needs good ground, like when he won his juvenile at Market Rasen. He hated the heavy ground when he was third up at Kelso (handicap hurdle debut) in October. He then went for a jumper's bumper at Newcastle and we were aiming him at a decent handicap before the season was cut short. He's still unexposed."

Novice: Tupelo Mississippi (b111): "He's a lovely horse, he won two bumpers up at Newcastle in February and March. He'll go hurdling this season and looks a very nice horse."

Alex Hales

British winners in 2019/20 (best seasonal tally)	**20 (career best)**
Impact Value in 2019/20	**1.57**
Percentage of rivals beaten in 2019/20	**60.33**
Timeform Run to Form % in 2019/20	**46.49**
Return at BSP in 2019/20	**+44.12**
Highest-rated horse in training	**Huntsman Son** Timeform Rating c140

Chaser: Huntsman Son (c140): "He'll be 10 soon, but he's still lightly raced and didn't do a lot wrong last season. I probably should have run him in the Grand Annual at Cheltenham as the ground went against him on the morning of the Close Brothers and he just didn't get home. He should really have won at Haydock after that, but he just got to the front too soon on that occasion. I think he's still got more to offer."

Hurdler: Stacey Sue (h105): "Still a maiden. She disappointed on handicap debut at Doncaster last time, but she came back all wrong from that and I still think she could be quite well handicapped off her current mark."

Novice: Millers Bank (h132): "He won two novice hurdles last season at Bangor and Market Rasen and, whilst he'll start back over hurdles, I think he'll be going 2m novice chasing this season. He's got an official BHA mark of 140 over hurdles, so he could be quite exciting."

Nicky Henderson

British winners in 2019/20 (best seasonal tally)	**118 (167)**
Impact Value in 2019/20	**2.13**
Percentage of rivals beaten in 2019/20	**63.14**
Timeform Run to Form % in 2019/20	**50.22**
Return at BSP in 2019/20	**+11.23**
Highest-rated horse in training	**Altior** Timeform Rating 175+

Chaser: Angels Breath (c150p): "Altior, Champ and Santini are obvious ones, but I am really looking forward to and hoping that Angels Breath will be back in action. He won his only two starts over fences very impressively, but unfortunately sustained a very nasty overreach when winning at Ascot which brought things to a halt. If he gets back this season he could be very exciting."

Hurdler: Glynn (h129p): "He's another we didn't see the full potential of last season as he only had one run over hurdles, though it was visually very impressive. He wasn't quite right after that and we were hoping to run him again in the spring, but the season was cut short and we couldn't. It will obviously be difficult having lost his novice status, but I hope he has a bright future over hurdles and eventually fences."

Novice: Pipesmoker (h125p): "He showed us loads of promise in both starts over hurdles and in his bumper the previous year. He's a big, imposing horse and we didn't mind not winning a novice hurdle with him last season as this will give him another full year as a novice. I think he has a very bright future."

Philip Hobbs

British winners in 2019/20 (best seasonal tally)	**75 (134)**
Impact Value in 2019/20	**1.55**
Percentage of rivals beaten in 2019/20	**60.76**
Timeform Run to Form % in 2019/20	**48.21**
Return at BSP in 2019/20	**-99.26**
Highest-rated horse in training	**Defi du Seuil** Timeform Rating c169

Chaser: Deise Aba (c143): "He was improving with experience during 2019/20 (won handicap at Sandown and good fifth in Kim Muir at Cheltenham) and could take a decent staying handicap chase this season."

Hurdler: Pile Up (Four-year-old unraced gelding by Yeats out of Full of Fruit): "Pile Up has just arrived in our yard from Ireland. He's a close relative of Pileon and had a good reputation with Tom Keating before the point to points were abandoned. It is possible his name might change before he runs."

Novice: Sporting John (h143): "He was unbeaten [in three starts] before the Cheltenham Festival and came back into the unsaddling enclosure after the Ballymore moving very oddly behind, although he was fine again very quickly. I think we can forgive him one blip and he could be a high-class novice chaser."

Anthony Honeyball

British winners in 2019/20 (best seasonal tally)	**36 (career best)**
Impact Value in 2019/20	**2.21**
Percentage of rivals beaten in 2019/20	**63.58**
Timeform Run to Form % in 2019/20	**53.17**
Return at BSP in 2019/20	**+26.41**
Highest-rated horse in training	**Sam Brown** Timeform Rating c147

Chaser: Sojourn (c128): "A lovely big horse that jumps very well and has never been out of the frame. He acts on any ground, still seems on a sensible mark and could make up in to a high-class handicapper. He's been a big, weak horse and is still improving in that regard."

Hurdler: Kid Commando (h129p): "He'll definitely stay hurdling and has a big engine. He was a staying-on third in a Grade 2 novice hurdle last time out and will probably try a decent handicap hurdle early this season. Stepping up to 2½m and further will be a major positive as well and he acts on any ground."

Novice: Coquelicot (b105): "She improved with every race last season, although it would be easy to argue her last run and biggest win in Listed company was one run too many for a four-year-old in her first season racing. She's won her last three bumpers and is growing all the time, so I expect further improvement. She's already schooled on grass and ought to be a force to be reckoned with in mares' novice hurdle events—the Dawn Run at Cheltenham will be her ultimate target. She'll stay further than 2½m and will act on any ground."

Dr Richard Newland

British winners in 2019/20 (best seasonal tally)	**60 (career best)**
Impact Value in 2019/20	**1.68**
Percentage of rivals beaten in 2019/20	**59.09**
Timeform Run to Form % in 2019/20	**43.84**
Return at BSP in 2019/20	**+38.15**
Highest-rated horse in training	**Le Patriote** Timeform Rating h145

Chaser: Katpoli (c135): "Is still very young, but he's improved every season and I'd be hopeful there's even more to come from him over fences. I'm not sure whether we'll go back to 2½m with him. I have a feeling he might just be an out-and-out 2m horse."

Hurdler: Rikoboy (h117): "Still a maiden over hurdles, but he showed some decent form in juvenile contests in France and he'll stick to hurdling this season. He's better than he's shown to date."

Novice: Mr Muldoon (h128p): "He did very well over hurdles last season, winning three times. He'll be going novice chasing this season and, as a dual winning pointer, we expect he'll improve further for the switch to fences."

Paul Nicholls

British winners in 2019/20 (best seasonal tally)	**96 (171)**
Impact Value in 2019/20	**1.68**
Percentage of rivals beaten in 2019/20	**62.29**
Timeform Run to Form % in 2019/20	**48.99**
Return at BSP in 2019/20	**+26.01**
Highest-rated horse in training	**Cyrname** Timeform Rating c174

Chaser: Saint Sonnet (c142p): "A listed winner over hurdles in France before winning his sole novice chase start, he then joined us and won at Catterick before running an eye-catching race in the Marsh at Cheltenham. We haven't by any means seen the best of him yet."

Hurdler: McFabulous (h142p): "A high-class bumper horse. He took time to get things right over hurdles but came good when winning the EBF Final at Kempton in March. He stays very well and could make up into a Stayers' Hurdle horse one day."

Novice: Pic D'Orhy (h148): "A horse who boasted top-class form in France before joining us and demonstrated that talent when winning the Betfair Hurdle at Newbury. We have been patient with him to save him for chasing and we are looking forward to him this season."

David Pipe

British winners in 2019/20 (best seasonal tally)	**64 (134)**
Impact Value in 2019/20	**1.65**
Percentage of rivals beaten in 2019/20	**57.32**
Timeform Run to Form % in 2019/20	**43.99**
Return at BSP in 2019/20	**+65.9**
Highest-rated horse in training	**Ramses De Teillee** Timeform Rating c151

Chaser: Ramses de Teillee (c151): "He had a fantastic season novice hurdling, winning a couple of graded events. The plan is to go chasing again this season, though we'll keep hurdling as an option. He's already a wonderful staying chaser and the long-term aim will be the Grand National."

Hurdler: Kepagge (h129+): "Won a bumper impressively at Chepstow and did very well over hurdles, producing a very good performance at Doncaster last time. His mark of 135 looks okay and you would hope he can be competitive in some decent handicap hurdles this winter."

Novice: Martinhal (b101+): "Ex-Irish pointer who put up a decent performance on his stable debut in a bumper at Huntingdon. He gives the impression he could develop into a lovely staying novice hurdler this season."

Jamie Snowden

British winners in 2019/20 (best seasonal tally)	**46 (career best)**
Impact Value in 2019/20	**1.58**
Percentage of rivals beaten in 2019/20	**57.82**
Timeform Run to Form % in 2019/20	**42.23**
Return at BSP in 2019/20	**-1.94**
Highest-rated horse in training	**Hogan's Height** Timeform Rating c142

Chaser: Pacify (h133): "Officially he'll be a novice, but he did really well over hurdles last season and we've been looking forward to seeing him over fences. We think he could be a smart chaser."

Hurdler: Thebannerkingrebel (h138): "Progressed nicely over hurdles last season, winning three times prior to disappointing in the Betfair Hurdle at Newbury (handicap debut), there should still be more to come from him as a hurdler."

Novice: Kiltealy Briggs (h130): "Managed to win twice over hurdles last season, but has long since had the size and scope to make a chaser and that's the road he'll be going down."

Harry Whittington

British winners in 2019/20 (best seasonal tally)	**30 (career best)**
Impact Value in 2019/20	**1.61**
Percentage of rivals beaten in 2019/20	**56.49**
Timeform Run to Form % in 2019/20	**38.75**
Return at BSP in 2019/20	**+17.42**
Highest-rated horse in training	**Saint Calvados** Timeform Rating c165

Chaser: Simply The Betts (c154p): "Going left handed seems important to him. He jumped aggressively left when beaten at Kempton last season, so I think we'll stick to left-handed courses this time round. He was very strong at the finish when he won at the Cheltenham Festival, but we'll stick to 2½m at the beginning of the season and aim him at something like the Old Roan Chase at Aintree. He's very versatile in terms of ground and should have more improvement in him."

Hurdler: Doc Picked Me (Unraced four-year-old gelding by Getaway out of Hard Luck): "I know he'll officially be a novice and I'm breaking the rules slightly, but I'm looking forward to this horse. He's named after Derek O'Connor, who literally did as the name suggests. He's bred to stay well but he's a precocious sort and has shown plenty of speed at home. He's very exciting."

Novice: Young Bull (h130p): "A very talented horse, who went way beyond our expectations over hurdles, winning three, and he didn't get the run of the race in what were terrible conditions at Warwick on his final start. He's a big, strapping type with a huge engine and he'll start off in novice handicap chases. If he proves to be as good as we think he could be then hopefully he'll take in some of the more prestigious novice races before the end of the season."

RISING STARS

Sam Allwood

Base	**Church Farm, Shropshire**
First Full Licence	**2019**
First Jumps Winner	**Mantou** Sedgefield 23/04/2018
Total Winners	**10**
Best Horse Trained	**Sheneededtherun** Timeform Rating c128

Unearthing a talented trainer or jockey that has escaped the attentions of the wider betting public can be just as vital as identifying a similarly overlooked horse. Sam Allwood was a successful point-to-point/hunter chase rider and has been training such horses from his Shropshire base since 2010, landing his first winner under Rules in 2018. It wasn't until the summer of the following year that Allwood gained his full National Hunt licence but, if 2019/20 is anything to go by, he's a trainer likely to garner plenty of attention in coming seasons.

A former employee of Philip Hobbs and Robert Alner, Allwood had only 11 horses in training last season, though his overall record was impressive, boasting nine winners from just 43 runners and a strike rate of 21%. The nine victories were shared out amongst three horses, all of whom returned a level-stakes profit, the most notable of which was stable flagbearer, Sheneededtherun. The daughter of Kayf Tara, acquired from Ben Pauling for just £6,500 in May 2019, won four of her six starts in 2019/20, earning £28,369.18 prize money and improving 25 lb on Timeform's scale.

A trainer's ability to improve a horse that has been with another well-thought-of yard is a trait that should always be viewed positively, but just as important is the knack of training a horse to peak at just the right time, a skill that Allwood displayed perfectly with Jobsonfire. He failed to make much of an impact in a trio of novice hurdles but progressed markedly when switched to staying handicaps, winning all three of his starts in that sphere and improving from 93 to 112p.

Reasons beyond anyone's control stopped Allwood from achieving more in 2019/20, but the upside is that he'll still have runners with something to offer and, with the distinct possibility of the yard attracting new recruits, Sam Allwood is a name well worthy of note in 2020/21.

Fergus Gillard

Attached Stable	**David Pipe**
First Ride	**2018**
First Winner	**No No Cardinal** Worcester 25/04/2019
Total Winners	**13**
Best Jumps Horse Ridden	**Main Fact** Timeform Rating h145+

Nobody would have wanted the jumps season to end as abruptly as it did but especially not Fergus Gillard. The young amateur jockey was on the crest of a wave when racing—and just about everything else—was brought to a premature halt by the Covid-19 pandemic. In the two weeks prior to the cessation, Gillard had ridden four winners and a second from just seven rides. For good measure he also partnered a double at Buckfastleigh on what turned out to be the final day of the point-to-point season, Sunday March 15.

Although he only rode his first winner just over a year ago, Gillard is not a newcomer to racing. His father Mark is a trainer and his mother, Pippa, a former world champion polo player who played for England no less than 40 times. Fergus, who has been schooling horses from the tender age of six, and his older brother Theo—now a conditional jockey attached to the Donald McCain stable—both started off in pony racing, with Fergus enjoying considerable success on a pony called Veno Star. Since turning his attention to the National Hunt game, Fergus has also built up a good rapport with a number of horses, notably his father's No No Cardinal (on whom he boasts a 100% record) and Main Fact. Indeed, that pair between them are responsible for almost half (six) of Gillard's total of 13 winners to date but dig a little deeper into the stats and you find some much more revealing ones. Those 13 winners came from just 59 rides giving him a very healthy strike rate of 22% (and a level stakes profit on his rides of £25.83). Of all the riders to have had more than 50 rides in the latest season, only four (Nico de Boinville, Barry Geraghty, David Maxwell and Joe Colliver) can boast a better strike rate than young Gillard. Even more impressive than that is the fact that just over 50% of his rides finished in the frame.

Gillard, who turned 18 at the end of April, only rode for a total of four trainers last term but he is sure to be in high demand, especially as he is still eligible to claim 7 lb. He seems destined for big things in the coming seasons.

Conor McNamara

Attached Stable	**Gavin Cromwell**
First Ride	**2016**
First Winner	**Offshore Oscar** Killarney 24/08/2018
Total Winners	**41**
Best Jumps Horses Ridden	**Wolf Prince/Charlie Stout** Timeform Rating h140/c140

"Try to get to the winning line I'd say." That's Conor McNamara's main aim for 2020. That self-effacing quip came in the immediate aftermath of McNamara misjudging the finishing post aboard Peaches And Cream at Leopardstown's Christmas meeting. It wasn't a costly error, however, as his mount had done enough at that stage and held on for a half-length victory. A lesson learned and a winner in front of both the RTE and Racing TV cameras—all in all not a bad day at the office for a fledgling jockey.

From Rathkeale in county Limerick, it is fair to say that Conor was destined for a career in racing. His father Eric is a successful trainer (probably best known for his three Kerry National wins) and his older brother Emmet is a former champion apprentice in Ireland who won the Derby on the Aidan O'Brien-trained Serpentine this year. Conor himself has spent three summers with Dermot Weld as well as six months with Robbie McNamara and rode, unsuccessfully, as an apprentice on the Flat. His elusive first winner under Rules (rode four winners in pony races) came aboard his father's Offshore Oscar in a handicap hurdle at Killarney.

Four more winners would follow in 2018/19 but things really took off last term and most of that is down to his link-up with Gavin Cromwell.

Of course, Cromwell wasn't the only trainer in Ireland to notice McNamara's talents. Conor had rides for a total of 44 trainers in Ireland last term. He rides out two days a week for Willie Mullins and the Champion Trainer has used him in several big handicaps, including the Martin Pipe at the Cheltenham Festival, and also supplied him with a big win on Ifyoucatchmenow in the Grand National Trial at Punchestown. His biggest winner to date came aboard Charlie Stout in the valuable Dan & Joan Moore Memorial Handicap Chase at Fairyhouse on his first ride for Shane Nolan.

With the likes of Cromwell and Mullins in his corner it seems that the only way is up for McNamara. He's excellent value for his 5-lb claim, has no weight issues and—with more than 300 rides under National Hunt Rules under his belt in the last two seasons—he also has plenty of experience.

Eoin Walsh

Attached Stable	**Noel Meade**
First Ride	**2019**
First Winner	**Calicojack** Down Royal 06/05/19
Total Winners	**27**
Best Jumps Horses Ridden	**Snow Falcon/Tout Est Permis** Timeform Rating c154

"He's a nice lad from Cork and he rides very well" were the first words we heard about Eoin Walsh after he had managed to cajole Noel Meade's Calicojack to victory in a maiden hurdle at Down Royal in early-2019/20. That was just Eoin's second ride under Rules and, although he had to wait until August to ride his second winner, it was pretty much onward and upwards from that point.

More winners followed, including a double at Down Royal on St. Stephen's Day, and if the betting public hadn't yet noticed what great value Walsh was for his 7-lb claim—that pair won at 9/1 and 16/1—then it wasn't being overlooked by his employer, or by Gigginstown House Stud, who used Walsh to excellent effect on Ice Cold Soul in a handicap chase at Thurles in January and Ificudiwud in a handicap hurdle at Fairyhouse In February. The latter success put Walsh on 14 winners for the season, but the best was still to come as all three parties combined again to land the Leinster National at Naas the following month with Cap York, Walsh's strength and claim proving crucial as Cap York wore down the long-time leader late on.

A trip to Cheltenham followed and, after guiding Tout Est Permis to third in the Pertemps Final and Snow Falcon to a mid-field finish in the Brown Advisory & Merriebelle Stable Plate, it was only bad luck that denied Walsh a fairytale first Cheltenham Festival success when Column of Fire departed at the last when looking the most likely winner in the Martin Pipe Conditional Jockeys' Handicap Hurdle.

It would have been understandable had the 'nice lad from Cork' taken time to get over such a cruel twist of fate, but any notions that it would have a negative impact on him were quickly brushed aside when he returned to the winner's enclosure the following day after an all-action display on board Barbary Master at Navan.

Walsh finished 2019/20 with 17 winners from 121 rides (he also rode 13 seconds) and, though his claim has been cut to 5 lb, the benefit of further experience coupled with the support of two powerhouses means that Walsh will be a rider to follow for 2020/21 and beyond.

ANTE-POST BETTING

Timeform Racing Analyst Ben Fearnley takes a look at the markets for some of the highlights in the National Hunt calendar and picks out his best value bets...

Finding a particularly strong piece of form that can be followed almost blindly for a season or so is the holy grail for many punters, especially if a particular race can be pinpointed before the market cottons on. An obvious example of such a race was the 2011 Supreme, featuring the likes of Al Ferof (peak Timeform rating 171+), the ill-fated Spirit Son (159p), Sprinter Sacre (192p), Cue Card (182), Rathlin (160) and Zaidpour (162), though the front trio in the 2016 renewal of the same race—Altior (180p), Min (176) and Buveur d'Air (170)—weren't a bad bunch, either. The feeling is that the 2020 Supreme—featuring two of our *Fifty*, Shishkin and Chantry House—will work out well, and the most recent running of the Albert Bartlett also appeals as notably strong form in the context of recent renewals, particularly so far as the front four are concerned. Indeed, two of that quartet—along with six others—are put up as ante-post selections in the following pages.

Ladbrokes Trophy

The top of the Ladbrokes Trophy market is packed with second-season chasers and, given that three of the last four renewals have gone to horses in that group (**De Rasher Counter**, Total Recall and Native River) it's worth focusing on similarly lightly-raced types who haven't yet shown their all. After winning at the Festival it's probably no real surprise that the BHA handicapper has been conservative with marks for the likes of **Champ** (161) and **Imperial Aura** (157), but he has done connections of **Copperhead** a small favour by dropping him to 153 after a poor run behind the former in the RSA. That was obviously disappointing (well beaten when falling heavily at the last) but there were clear mitigating circumstances, not least the overall form of the Colin Tizzard yard during Festival week. Also, Copperhead was by no means the first horse to bomb out after putting up a big effort on barely raceable ground at Ascot in mid-February, and there's a good chance he simply hadn't had enough time to get over his impressive Reynoldstown victory three and a half weeks on. One bad run doesn't undo the considerable progress he'd made during his novice campaign as a whole, and it's worth noting how well he

Copperhead developed into a smart novice chaser last season

took to Newbury when winning a C&D handicap in impressive fashion in late-December. Though connections eventually opted for the RSA over the National Hunt Chase at the Festival, Copperhead's future lies over marathon trips and he could be in for another productive season, the Ladbrokes Trophy and the Welsh National—a double completed by Tizzard with Native River in 2016/17—both likely to be right up his street. A potential fly in the ointment is **Topofthegame**. The case for thinking he'll be a force in the coming season is outlined in our Gold Cup preview later in the article and this could well be an ideal starting point for him, the lack of handicap openings for top staying chasers in the autumn well documented, while trainer Paul Nicholls is certainly not the type to turn down a crack at a big pot when he's got the right sort of horse.

SELECTIONS: Topofthegame (7/1) and Copperhead (14/1)

King George VI Chase

Colin Tizzard's poor Festival in 2020 forms the basis of our next bet, too—**Lostintranslation** for the King George, though in contrast to many of his stable companions he actually ran to form at Cheltenham, tanking through the Gold Cup for a long way before being outstayed by **Al Boum Photo** and **Santini**. Considering the cloud hanging over the yard during that week, Lostintranslation's effort arguably enhanced his overall reputation, and he's likely to be a big factor in the top staying contests in the coming season, tracks such as Haydock and, in particular, Kempton more suited to his skillset than the Gold Cup C&D. That last point made his run in last season's King George all the more puzzling at the time (never travelling with his usual verve and making some notable—and uncharacteristic—late jumping errors), but he was subsequently reported to have suffered a breathing problem, making the run perfectly forgivable, particularly given that a pre-Gold Cup wind operation seemed to work the oracle. Lostintranslation is currently the same price as Champ and Santini, neither of whom will be ideally suited by the test that Kempton offers, while he holds a slight class edge on ratings over current favourite **Clan des Obeaux**. The other horse that stands out as being overpriced is **Cyrname**. Yes, his form is very Ascot-centric and, like Lostintranslation, he was disappointing in the 2019 renewal, but three miles round Kempton should suit in theory (kept to right-handed tracks) and there's a chance that his defeat of Altior in November—on very soft ground—left a bit of a mark on both horses for the remainder of the season, Cyrname never really going with his usual zest on either of his subsequent starts, including when taking a heavy fall back at Ascot in February. Despite Paul Nicholls issuing a very positive bulletin on Cyrname later that month, he's as big as 16/1 for the 2020 King George, worth remembering he was sent off 5/4 favourite for the 2019 renewal.

SELECTIONS: Lostintranslation (8/1) and Cyrname (16/1)

RSA Chase

Minella Indo went agonisingly close—1.06 in-running on the Betfair Exchange in fact—to doing the Albert Bartlett/RSA Chase double for the first time since Bobs Worth in 2012. Though he was eventually collared by Champ in the dying strides, he along with Allaho (third) showed once again how useful a guide the staying novice hurdle race is to the chasing equivalent, and it's well worth focusing on this year's Albert Bartlett when taking a long-range look at the RSA, particularly as current favourite **Envoi Allen** has many other options. Given he's still a raw, gawky individual, it was hard not to be taken with how well **Monkfish** dug in to win the latest Albert Bartlett, especially as he'd hardly had to battle when winning his previous two starts in Ireland by wide margins. He's clearly built to take well to chasing and seems sure to be even better with another summer under his belt, odds of 10/1 for this season's RSA making appeal given how obvious a fit he seems for the race. There's a chance that Monkfish will renew rivalries with **Latest Exhibition** (second in the Albert Bartlett) and **Fury Road** (third) before the next Festival, all three likely to be contesting the same sort of races in Ireland throughout the season, and the hope is that he can confirm himself best of the bunch once again.

SELECTION: Monkfish (10/1)

Defi du Seuil (right) on his way to victory in the Clarence House

Champion Chase

A number of our selections so far have come on the back of bookmakers overreacting to a poor run or two at the back-end of the previous season, perhaps no better example of that than **Defi du Seuil**'s current odds for the Champion Chase—as big as 14/1 at the time of writing. Admittedly, he lost his unbeaten record at the Festival in hugely disappointing fashion, essentially the first beaten in a field that had cut up significantly, but his current odds seem to almost ignore the good work he'd done prior to March, his sharp turn of foot on display when winning the Shloer, Tingle Creek and Clarence House—three of the key races in the division in the autumn/winter months. He's arguably got less to prove than **Altior** (an 8/1-chance), and while **Chacun Pour Soi** could simply be a better horse (very possible on what he did to Min at the Dublin Racing Festival) the gap between the two in the market is too big. In terms of novice prospects arriving on the scene, the Arkle was a pretty underwhelming affair in 2020, favourite **Notebook** not the only one to disappoint, but he was unbeaten prior to that and his previous form did take a boost with **Fakir d'Oudairies**—who he'd beaten at Leopardstown over Christmas—finishing second to **Put The Kettle On**. A buzzy type who has been known to bolt to post, Notebook is the type to improve as he matures, and as such is worth a small interest at long odds in an open-looking market.

SELECTIONS: Defi du Seuil (14/1) and Notebook (33/1)

Stayers' Hurdle

As is often the case, the vast majority of the Albert Bartlett field will probably end up over fences this season, one of the main reasons why the staying hurdle division is traditionally the weakest around, the finish of the most recent renewal of the Stayers' Hurdle resembling a high-end handicap more than a Grade 1 event. **Paisley Park** could well bounce back in 2021, reportedly suffering from an irregular heartbeat when down the field at Cheltenham, but he suddenly doesn't look as invincible as before, while the next two in the market—talented mares **Benie des Dieux** and **Honeysuckle**—will probably end up running against their own sex once again. Dual Pertemps winner **Sire du Berlais** could represent some new blood in the ranks, but he's quite a lazy type and the blinkers which sweetened him up last time aren't sure to work as well again. The one that really catches the eye in the betting is **Thyme Hill**, who was better than the result when fourth in the Albert Bartlett, the gap Richard Johnson was attempting to explore coming to the last closing at the last second. The

Thyme Hill (left) didn't enjoy the rub of the green in the Albert Bartlett

three that finished in front of him—Monkfish, Latest Exhibition and Fury Road—all reportedly have chasing on their agenda but that isn't guaranteed to be the case for Thyme Hill, his trainer making a point of stating that he's 'not the biggest' on more than one occasion. If he stays over hurdles, he'll surely be a major player in the top staying races in 2020/21, including the Stayers' Hurdle itself.

SELECTION: Thyme Hill (16/1)

Cheltenham Gold Cup

Nicky Henderson has now trained the runner-up in two of the last three runnings of the Gold Cup and one horse might well have been responsible—directly and indirectly—for both defeats. Directly, **Native River** turned away the strong-travelling Might Bite in the 2018 renewal, while indirectly his non-participation in the 2020 running (due to injury) changed the entire complexion of the race, in which **Santini** finished second. Without Native River forcing the issue the Gold Cup was not nearly so much of a stamina test as is often the case and, based on the way Santini stayed on after the last, he was the one most inconvenienced by the set-up. Granted more of a test Santini may well go one better in 2021, though he'll inevitably be facing some new opposition, not least from his stable-companion **Champ** and the horse Champ beat into second in the RSA, **Minella Indo**. We may also see Santini renew rivalry with the horse that got the better of him in that particular contest in 2019, **Topofthegame** (one of our *Fifty*), who missed last season due to an early injury. That RSA has worked out notably well, the third **Delta Work** winning a pair of Grade 1 races in Ireland last season before a respectable fifth behind **Al Boum Photo** at Cheltenham, and the recent news that Topofthegame is now back in training following his setback will be exciting for connections. Topofthegame—reportedly the tallest horse Nicholls has ever trained—is the type to be even better with time, still looking raw throughout much of his novice campaign. He clearly goes well at Cheltenham, finishing second in the Coral Cup on his final start over hurdles in 2017/18, and can hopefully make up for lost time this season.

SELECTION: Topofthegame (16/1)

LEADING JUMPS SIRES

There are many ways of measuring 'success' so far as a sire is concerned. The most commonly used is 'prize money earned', but so far as punters are concerned that's a decidedly blunt tool. And that's why this article aims to dig deeper in an attempt to highlight information that could prove useful in day-to-day punting.

The accompanying tables are based on results in the Britain and Ireland during the shortened 2019/20 season and, as such, some of the sample sizes are smaller than ideal, but at the same time there are undoubtedly some potentially useful snippets to be drawn from the data.

Overall

No Risk At All sits proudly at the top of the Overall table (all races, min 100 runners) by strike-rate and by an emphatic margin, too, pretty much one in four of his runners being successful in the latest season. To some extent, his numbers are skewed by the fact that his oldest progeny were only six in the latest season, and he therefore doesn't have dozens of exposed or deteriorating horses doing the rounds as yet, but at the same time it's hugely impressive that he's responsible for the Champion Hurdle winner Epatante and RSA third Allaho after only a few crops, whilst the likes of Gumball and Esprit du Large have also achieved a smart level of form. The Profit/Loss figure is flattering on account of Fleur Irlandais' 100/1 success in a handicap at Kempton, but there's less to argue with so far as his Percentage of Rivals Beaten % is concerned, that figure suggesting No Risk At All has been responsible for fewer duds than usual at this early stage of his stud career. One of his progeny worth looking out for is the Tom Lacey-trained **L'Incorrigible**, the impressive winner of a junior bumper at Warwick before Christmas and possessing more physical scope than most winners of such races.

The now-deceased Poliglote owes his position in the table largely to the performances of a few well-established ones, the surprise Champion Chase winner Politologue being the best of them, though he was also represented in the latest season by fellow Festival winner Sire du Berlais, the most likeable Top Notch and the smart handicap chaser Capeland.

Further down the list, King's Theatre is still managing to produce household names despite having passed away in 2011, the RSA winner Champ being the pick of his final crop, his average rating of more than 106 (rising to almost 113 when confined to chasers only) worthy of a special mention given the ageing nature of his progeny. Authorized is another stallion who'll have fewer representatives in years to come, having been sold to the Turkish Jockey Club at the back-end of 2019, but whilst Tiger Roll edges further towards the end of a truly staggering career there's another potential jumping superstar to look forward to from the 2007 Derby winner, **Goshen** looking for all the world as though he can go to the top of the tree in the hurdling division.

Some of the names in the lower reaches of the table are more surprising than others. Oscar's numbers are swayed to some extent by the sheer volume of his progeny on the racecourse but it was still a bit disappointing that he had so few up-and-comers in the latest season. That said, Lisnagar Oscar did keep the Stayers' Hurdle in the family after Paisley Park, another son of Oscar, fluffed his lines. Mahler is another sire with huge numbers of runners over jumps, and that despite his oldest progeny being no more than 10 in the latest season. Even at this relatively early stage of his stallion career, it's clear that his progeny are more interesting over fences than hurdles, a chase strike-rate of over 13% in 2019/20 contrasting sharply with a strike-rate of less than 7% over hurdles—the contrast is similarly stark over a much longer period of time—novices such as Commanche Red, Deise Aba and Annie MC contributing healthily to the chase numbers and Chris's Dream improving sufficiently to earn himself a crack at the Gold Cup. Finally, a mention must go to Scorpion, who was responsible for Might Bite in his first crop but has since been by some way the single-most disappointing mass market National Hunt sire around. Riders Onthe Storm was comfortably his highest-profile winner in the latest season, but overall it was yet another campaign of underwhelming results from the son of Montjeu.

2019/20 Top Jumps Sires in Britain & Ireland by Strike Rate (min 100 runners, all races)

Sire	BestHorse	Runners	Winners	SR	IV	PL	Avg Rating	PRB
NO RISK AT ALL (FR)	EPATANTE (FR)	104	25	24.04	2.17	105.71	106.26	60.37
POLIGLOTE	POLITOLOGUE (FR)	110	21	19.09	1.7	33.09	111.98	55.35
NATHANIEL (IRE)	CONCERTISTA (FR)	118	22	18.64	1.7	16.86	92.32	56.88
BORN TO SEA (IRE)	ASPIRE TOWER (IRE)	132	24	18.18	1.68	-4.03	98.11	57.48
SAINT DES SAINTS (FR)	SAINT CALVADOS (FR)	181	31	17.13	1.4	-51.6	109.61	59.12
GREAT PRETENDER (IRE)	BENIE DES DIEUX (FR)	142	24	16.9	1.49	-31.1	102.17	56.73
KING'S THEATRE (IRE)	CHAMP (IRE)	438	72	16.44	1.32	-70.08	106.66	54.21
NETWORK (GER)	DELTA WORK (FR)	202	33	16.34	1.45	-63.43	105.09	57.5
AUTHORIZED (IRE)	GOSHEN (FR)	201	32	15.92	1.32	-53.32	105.94	57.12
CLOUDINGS (IRE)	VINTAGE CLOUDS (IRE)	110	17	15.45	1.42	-17.8	95.4	52.94
SHANTOU (USA)	BEWARE THE BEAR (IRE)	557	86	15.44	1.45	-44.79	98.85	57.13
BEAT HOLLOW	MINELLA INDO (IRE)	243	36	14.81	1.44	-54.62	91.11	52.76
MARTALINE	MARRACUDJA (FR)	317	45	14.2	1.3	-86.76	101.13	52.62
BLACK SAM BELLAMY (IRE)	SAM BROWN	383	54	14.1	1.23	-66.76	94.26	52.54
SADDLER MAKER (IRE)	BRISTOL DE MAI (FR)	107	15	14.02	1.24	-37.02	115.35	59.88
RIP VAN WINKLE (IRE)	POINT OF PRINCIPLE (IRE)	101	14	13.86	1.29	-25.21	90.36	51.87
SULAMANI (IRE)	HONEYSUCKLE	306	42	13.73	1.18	2.28	88.44	50.32
PASSING GLANCE	DASHEL DRASHER	171	23	13.45	1.2	31.6	92.52	55.5
GOLD WELL	EMITOM (IRE)	773	103	13.32	1.25	-176.83	95.64	54.92

ZOFFANY (IRE)	SIR PSYCHO (IRE)	129	17	13.18	1.38	-9.4	92.75	52.29
MALINAS (GER)	MISTER MALARKY	228	30	13.16	1.23	3.35	91.7	56.1
WINGED LOVE (IRE)	RAVENHILL (IRE)	215	28	13.02	1.2	1.13	93.68	48.79
DEFINITE ARTICLE	DEFINITLY RED (IRE)	154	20	12.99	1.08	-30.88	97.11	50.14
CHAMPS ELYSEES	TURNPIKE TRIP	165	21	12.73	1.13	-58.46	92.96	51.27
FAME AND GLORY	EMBITTERED (IRE)	387	49	12.66	1.3	-192.6	91.53	59.08
MASTERCRAFTSMAN (IRE)	SCARAMANGA (IRE)	245	31	12.65	1.22	25.44	93.2	50.06
SHIROCCO (GER)	ROCK THE KASBAH (IRE)	438	55	12.56	1.21	-78.55	88.62	51.19
MIDNIGHT LEGEND	MIDNIGHT SHADOW	541	67	12.38	1.04	-67.01	95.84	50.11
ELUSIVE PIMPERNEL (USA)	EX PATRIOT (IRE)	154	19	12.34	1.41	-56.78	90.96	54.39
VOIX DU NORD (FR)	KEMBOY (FR)	115	14	12.17	1.03	-57.95	114.87	53.15
CALIFET (FR)	CILAOS EMERY (FR)	115	14	12.17	1.14	52.49	88.18	45.73
KAYF TARA	SECRET INVESTOR	576	69	11.98	1.06	14.87	97.53	51.11
SEPTEMBER STORM (GER)	STORM CONTROL (IRE)	151	18	11.92	1.08	-41.4	89.69	50.72
BENEFICIAL	TOP VILLE BEN (IRE)	695	82	11.8	1.07	-46.23	95.1	50.59
MULTIPLEX	BOLDMERE	182	21	11.54	1.09	-20.19	89.92	49.98
ROBIN DES CHAMPS (FR)	COLUMN OF FIRE (IRE)	324	37	11.42	1.05	-150.22	93.06	48.57
FLEMENSFIRTH (USA)	LOSTINTRANSLATION (IRE)	824	93	11.29	1.04	-226.25	99.65	52.5
GETAWAY (GER)	GETABIRD (IRE)	877	99	11.29	1.11	-345.03	89.74	51.48
KAPGARDE (FR)	CLAN DES OBEAUX (FR)	267	30	11.24	0.98	-135.01	101.25	53.36
FRUITS OF LOVE (USA)	SIMPLY NED (IRE)	125	14	11.2	1.05	4	90.98	49.67
AL NAMIX (FR)	PETIT MOUCHOIR (FR)	117	13	11.11	0.91	-74.77	104.83	56.68
ARAKAN (USA)	THEBANNERKINGREBEL (IRE)	283	31	10.95	1.03	-77.63	94.21	51.11
WESTERNER	TOTAL RECALL (IRE)	727	79	10.87	0.97	-232.31	97.11	50.63
KALANISI (IRE)	KALASHNIKOV (IRE)	416	45	10.82	1.05	-73.07	93.05	48.59
YEATS (IRE)	BRAVE EAGLE (IRE)	814	88	10.81	1.04	-275.33	93.28	51.23
MILAN	SANTINI	998	107	10.72	1	-367.88	95	51.63
WELL CHOSEN	CHOSEN MATE (IRE)	140	15	10.71	1.08	-64.33	100.22	53.03
PRESENTING	BALLYOISIN (IRE)	883	94	10.65	1	-272.78	95.02	51.66
JEREMY (USA)	MISTER FISHER (IRE)	569	60	10.54	1.1	-188.19	91.12	52.53
DUBAI DESTINATION (USA)	ELEGANT ESCAPE (IRE)	278	29	10.43	0.97	-137.31	96.31	51.74
STOWAWAY	PALOMA BLUE (IRE)	913	95	10.41	0.98	-410.07	96.36	53.06
COURT CAVE (IRE)	MISTER WHITAKER (IRE)	620	63	10.16	0.99	-201.77	90.01	49.26
CRAIGSTEEL	WHOLESTONE (IRE)	231	23	9.96	0.87	-115.98	94.72	50.09
CANFORD CLIFFS (IRE)	BEAT THE JUDGE (IRE)	111	11	9.91	0.93	-44.64	93.08	54.68
HIGH CHAPARRAL (IRE)	ALTIOR (IRE)	162	16	9.88	0.97	-69.94	88.6	49.53
SHOLOKHOV (IRE)	SHISHKIN (IRE)	173	17	9.83	0.95	-76.95	87.72	49.6
MOUNTAIN HIGH (IRE)	STONEY MOUNTAIN (IRE)	214	21	9.81	0.99	-60.39	89.33	47.07
MOUNT NELSON	PENHILL	102	10	9.8	0.87	-44.85	90.3	44.43
MOROZOV (USA)	SPYGLASS HILL (IRE)	185	18	9.73	0.92	10.22	86.59	44.49
DOYEN (IRE)	BATTLEOVERDOYEN (IRE)	422	41	9.72	0.94	-142.9	92.25	51.05

POET'S VOICE	LISP (IRE)	114	11	9.65	0.96	-66.31	92.62	56.43
BRIAN BORU	SUB LIEUTENANT (IRE)	273	26	9.52	0.78	-29.55	93.75	48.24
OSCAR (IRE)	LISNAGAR OSCAR (IRE)	874	83	9.5	0.92	-357.57	95.07	50.88
MAHLER	CHRIS'S DREAM (IRE)	764	72	9.42	0.88	-270.52	90.12	48.88
ASK	ASK DILLON (IRE)	290	27	9.31	0.95	-116.59	91.7	51.73
ARCADIO (GER)	HARDLINE (IRE)	486	45	9.26	0.91	-195.98	91.36	44.92
SCHIAPARELLI (GER)	RONALD PUMP	154	14	9.09	0.81	-26.18	93.67	49.88
TOUCH OF LAND (FR)	MOMUS (IRE)	111	10	9.01	0.87	-47.97	83.54	54.33
SIR PERCY	PRESENTING PERCY	135	12	8.89	0.82	-49.03	91.39	49.78
PAPAL BULL	THE JAM MAN (IRE)	114	10	8.77	0.89	-14.73	84.88	43.53
GALILEO (IRE)	SUPASUNDAE	224	19	8.48	0.82	-108.31	93.03	46.61
VINNIE ROE (IRE)	VINNDICATION (IRE)	239	20	8.37	0.71	-108.41	90.92	48.35
TRANS ISLAND	REDFORD ROAD	180	15	8.33	0.82	-71.63	89.45	51.2
LAWMAN (FR)	PLAY THE GAME (IRE)	110	9	8.18	0.83	-47.51	89.6	45.16
MEDICEAN	MELON	111	9	8.11	0.72	-52.13	88.54	47.97
GOLAN (IRE)	CAPTAIN CHAOS (IRE)	114	9	7.89	0.8	-40.5	92.26	44.57
GAMUT (IRE)	ROAD TO RESPECT (IRE)	102	8	7.84	0.68	-54.25	96.24	44.74
TEOFILO (IRE)	PEARL OF THE WEST (IRE)	128	10	7.81	0.78	-44.68	84.71	46.35
TIKKANEN (USA)	TIKKANEN EXPRESS (IRE)	117	9	7.69	0.67	-35.25	88.19	43.98
DR MASSINI (IRE)	DR MIKEY (IRE)	143	11	7.69	0.64	-71	87.03	47.5
SANS FRONTIERES (IRE)	JASON THE MILITANT (IRE)	118	9	7.63	0.78	-55.8	84.03	42.75
SCORPION (IRE)	RIDERS ONTHE STORM (IRE)	727	55	7.57	0.72	-433.59	88.8	46.84
BIG BAD BOB (IRE)	EIGHT AND BOB	119	9	7.56	0.84	-68.61	84.14	48.74
DYLAN THOMAS (IRE)	NUTS WELL	198	14	7.07	0.74	-94.7	84.96	45.02
FAIR MIX (IRE)	SOUTHFIELD STONE	222	14	6.31	0.58	-123.98	85.62	40.38
ROBIN DES PRES (FR)	ROBIN DES FORET (IRE)	233	14	6.01	0.55	-105	85.6	45.02
SIXTIES ICON	BUILDMEUPBUTTERCUP	122	7	5.74	0.55	-48.17	85.36	46.85

Hurdlers

Unsurprisingly, most of those towards the top of the hurdlers table (minimum 75 runners) had fewer representatives than the more established National Hunt sires such as Shantou, Midnight Legend, Gold Well and Shirocco, but a strike-rate of more than 16% for Shantou was noteworthy—he wasn't responsible for many standout performers but had plenty of maiden/novice winners as well as numerous mid-range handicappers that contributed to the total. Shirocco is another sire that lacked a big-name representative last season, but he does have the likes of *Fifty* representatives **Lieutenant Rocco**, **Highway One O Two** and **Rock On Rocco** to potentially improve his figures next season. Nathaniel is obviously marketed as a Flat sire but, following on from such as Sadler's Wells, Montjeu and Authorized before him, it hasn't taken him long to establish himself as an excellent source of good-quality hurdlers, bagging a Festival double courtesy of the Willie Mullins pair Concertista and Burning Victory and also responsible for the Triumph fourth Navajo Pass. Nathaniel's oldest runners were only six in the latest season and it's safe to assume he'll be responsible for lots of hurdling winners in years to come.

2019/20 Top 25 Jumps Sires in Britain & Ireland by Strike Rate (min 75 runners, Hurdles)

Sire	BestHorse	Runners	Winners	SR	IV	PL	Avg Rating	PRB
GREAT PRETENDER (IRE)	BENIE DES DIEUX (FR)	79	16	20.25	1.83	-0.75	101.2	60.97
NATHANIEL (IRE)	CONCERTISTA (FR)	100	20	20	1.76	14.36	95.15	57.51
POUR MOI (IRE)	WOLF PRINCE (IRE)	87	17	19.54	1.87	30.91	96.59	60.51
SAINT DES SAINTS (FR)	ELFILE (FR)	94	18	19.15	1.66	-35.5	108.14	62.49
BORN TO SEA (IRE)	ASPIRE TOWER (IRE)	112	21	18.75	1.81	6.52	100.18	56.87
SHANTOU (USA)	THE STORYTELLER (IRE)	334	54	16.17	1.69	-8.95	98.08	59.25
AUTHORIZED (IRE)	GOSHEN (FR)	146	23	15.75	1.46	-40.64	104.86	56.34
MARTALINE	AGRAPART (FR)	197	31	15.74	1.53	-69.39	102.97	55.45
CAPE CROSS (IRE)	LEONCAVALLO (IRE)	90	14	15.56	1.51	5.06	93.81	49.48
KING'S THEATRE (IRE)	WILLIAM HENRY (IRE)	157	24	15.29	1.42	-15.31	97.1	56.33
MALINAS (GER)	HARAMBE	144	21	14.58	1.39	-9.1	95.59	54.44
ARAKAN (USA)	THEBANNERKINGREBEL (IRE)	182	25	13.74	1.4	-11	94.35	52.23
MIDNIGHT LEGEND	SIR IVAN	279	38	13.62	1.29	-27.28	92.28	51.45
ZOFFANY (IRE)	SIR PSYCHO (IRE)	125	17	13.6	1.42	-5.4	93.03	53.11
SULAMANI (IRE)	HONEYSUCKLE	195	26	13.33	1.22	-2.31	86.79	50.02
FAME AND GLORY	EMBITTERED (IRE)	255	34	13.33	1.38	-118.37	98.13	61.17
GOLD WELL	EMITOM (IRE)	469	60	12.79	1.33	-165.1	93.89	56.03
SEPTEMBER STORM (GER)	EVERYBREATHYOUTAKE (IRE)	79	10	12.66	1.22	-31.65	89.89	47.38
MASTERCRAFTSMAN (IRE)	SCARAMANGA (IRE)	199	25	12.56	1.25	12.44	93.17	51.12
WINGED LOVE (IRE)	GLYNN (IRE)	80	10	12.5	1.38	-5.18	88.33	44.12
RIP VAN WINKLE (IRE)	POINT OF PRINCIPLE (IRE)	89	11	12.36	1.22	-21.13	89.64	51.65
SHIROCCO (GER)	HIGHWAY ONE O TWO (IRE)	248	30	12.1	1.18	-69.95	91.1	50.65
NETWORK (GER)	EASYWORK (FR)	91	11	12.09	1.22	-53.13	98.9	59.64
ROBIN DES CHAMPS (FR)	COLUMN OF FIRE (IRE)	191	23	12.04	1.17	-78.46	94.08	51.72
MULTIPLEX	SILVA ECLIPSE	128	15	11.72	1.17	1.95	87.51	50.96

Chasers

So far as chasers are concerned, Delta Work was again the flagbearer for Sprinter Sacre's sire Network last season, though a strike-rate nudging 20% (a figure which hardly falls even when a much longer period is taken into account) tells us he's anything but a one-trick pony. Acapella Bourgeois was also successful in graded company and the rapidly progressive Domaine de L'Isle notched three wins, including in a valuable handicap at Ascot. The lasting success of King's Theatre with chasers was touched on earlier in the article, whilst Arcadio is a sire that has an appreciably better record with chasers than hurdlers. Hardline, Simply The Betts and Crievehill were his star performers last season, Topofthecotswolds another to leave his hurdling form behind when switched to fences. Bearing this in mind, a couple of names worth looking out for next season are **Zanza** and **Up The Straight**, both sons of Arcadio that appeal as likely types to take their form to a higher level when sent chasing, whilst there's also the 2019 Ballymore third **Bright Forecast** to look forward to over fences, his return to the track delayed by a fibrillating heart last season.

2019/20 Top 25 Jumps Sires in Britain & Ireland by Strike Rate (min 75 runners, Chases)

Sire	BestHorse	Runners	Winners	SR	IV	PL	Avg Rating	PRB
NETWORK (GER)	DELTA WORK (FR)	101	20	19.8	1.59	-3.46	112.49	54.92
SULAMANI (IRE)	COPPERHEAD	79	15	18.99	1.42	33.72	96.44	55.41
BLACK SAM BELLAMY (IRE)	SAM BROWN	110	20	18.18	1.35	0.79	107.01	52.38
KING'S THEATRE (IRE)	CHAMP (IRE)	277	47	16.97	1.26	-55.27	112.78	52.58
DEFINITE ARTICLE	DEFINITLY RED (IRE)	86	13	15.12	1.11	-20.15	105.16	53.94
ARCADIO (GER)	HARDLINE (IRE)	115	17	14.78	1.24	-35.89	107.35	51.01
GOLD WELL	GALVIN (IRE)	240	35	14.58	1.12	-32.35	104.17	53.14
WINGED LOVE (IRE)	RAVENHILL (IRE)	111	16	14.41	1.15	19.71	99.92	53
GETAWAY (GER)	GETABIRD (IRE)	168	24	14.29	1.15	-19.77	102.94	53.67
KAPGARDE (FR)	CLAN DES OBEAUX (FR)	113	16	14.16	1.1	-32.24	111.93	52.17
MILAN	SANTINI	363	51	14.05	1.15	-42.48	103.98	51.35
YEATS (IRE)	BRAVE EAGLE (IRE)	189	26	13.76	1.05	-45.03	104.92	48.57
BENEFICIAL	TOP VILLE BEN (IRE)	410	56	13.66	1.12	26.34	101.29	52.41
DOYEN (IRE)	BATTLEOVERDOYEN (IRE)	126	17	13.49	1.03	-34.79	107.81	48.06
SHANTOU (USA)	BEWARE THE BEAR (IRE)	158	21	13.29	1.01	-22.24	108.04	51.51
FLEMENSFIRTH (USA)	LOSTINTRANSLATION (IRE)	317	42	13.25	1.06	39.29	109.31	49.02
KAYF TARA	SECRET INVESTOR	257	34	13.23	1.05	-1.18	105.42	51.69
MAHLER	CHRIS'S DREAM (IRE)	267	35	13.11	1.02	-81.56	100.26	49.13
PRESENTING	BALLYOISIN (IRE)	386	49	12.69	1.07	-143.65	103.32	50.04
KALANISI (IRE)	KALASHNIKOV (IRE)	103	13	12.62	0.97	-14.21	105.59	49.94
MARTALINE	MARRACUDJA (FR)	88	11	12.5	0.97	-0.7	107.79	46.7
MIDNIGHT LEGEND	MIDNIGHT SHADOW	220	26	11.82	0.85	-10.73	103.99	50.08
VOIX DU NORD (FR)	KEMBOY (FR)	94	11	11.7	0.95	-53.2	117.66	52.45
BRIAN BORU	SUB LIEUTENANT (IRE)	115	13	11.3	0.8	14.58	102.07	47.66
WESTERNER	TOTAL RECALL (IRE)	310	35	11.29	0.93	-60.79	106.16	50.91

SECTION 4

TIMEFORM'S VIEW

Chosen from the Timeform Formbook, here is Timeform's detailed analysis—compiled by our team of race reporters and supplemented by observations from Timeform's handicappers—of a selection of key races from both the Dublin Racing Festival at Leopardstown and the Cheltenham Festival.

LEOPARDSTOWN Saturday February 1

GOOD to SOFT

Nathaniel Lacy & Partners Solicitors '€50,000 Cheltenham Bonus For Stable Staff' Novice Hurdle (Golden Cygnet) (Grade 1)

Pos	*Btn*	*Horse*	*Age*	*Wgt*	*Eq*	*Trainer*	*Jockey*	*SP*
1		LATEST EXHIBITION (IRE)	7	11-10		Paul Nolan, Ireland	B. J. Cooper	7/2
2	2	COBBLER'S WAY (IRE)	6	11-10	(t)	Henry de Bromhead, Ireland	Rachael Blackmore	9/1
3	hd	LONGHOUSE POET (IRE)	6	11-10	(t)	Martin Brassil, Ireland	Mr J. J. Codd	6/1
4	3	FURY ROAD (IRE)	6	11-10	(t)	Gordon Elliott, Ireland	Davy Russell	9/4f
5	¾	ELIXIR D'AINAY (FR)	6	11-10		W. P. Mullins, Ireland	M. P. Walsh	3/1
6	4	ASSEMBLE	6	11-10	(t)	Joseph Patrick O'Brien, Ireland	J. J. Slevin	16/1
7	60	AIRCRAFT CARRIER (IRE)	5	11-8		Luke Comer, Ireland	R. A. Doyle	100/1
8	29	HOME BY THE LEE (IRE)	5	11-8	(h)	Joseph Patrick O'Brien, Ireland	Robbie Power	18/1

8 ran Race Time 5m 33.50 Closing Sectional (5.40f): 76.80s (106.6%) Winning Owner: Toberona Partnership

A Grade 1 staying novice in which most arrived having already posted useful figures and, while the run of the race probably favoured those that raced prominently, it's still form to view positively, Latest Exhibition running out a convincing winner in the end after the first 3 had jumped the last virtually in line; the pace was modest. **Latest Exhibition** upped in trip, didn't need to improve to follow up his recent Navan success in workmanlike fashion after 6 weeks off, again displaying a really likeable attitude; chased leaders, not fluent 4 out, third when ridden from 2 out, stayed on to lead run-in, asserted final 100 yds; bordering on smart, connections stated he may now head to the Albert Bartlett at Cheltenham and, while he may have less potential than some he's likely to face there, his straightforward nature and professional attitude are sure to stand him in good stead in a race that often develops into a slog. **Cobbler's Way** improved further but found one too good despite having the run of the race, though the manner in which he knuckled down again late on bodes well for the future and even longer trips; led, pressed 2 out, headed approaching last, rallied well near finish. **Longhouse Poet** improved again, just giving best to 2 stronger stayers at the trip having briefly held the advantage in the closing stages; chased leaders, took keen hold, not fluent sixth, ridden from 2 out, edged ahead briefly last, no extra final 100 yds. **Fury Road** ran well on form, though he didn't travel with the same verve that had characterised his previous wins in this sphere, the less testing conditions coupled with a modest pace leaving him vulnerable to those with a bit more tactical speed; chased leaders early, settled in touch, ridden approaching home turn, one paced; will stay 3m and remains open to improvement with that in mind. **Elixir d'Ainay** wasn't disgraced, running to a similar level as he had when runner-up at Naas in January despite his early exuberance counting against him late on; close up, took strong hold, shaken up from 2 out, no extra from last; remains open to improvement. **Assemble** back under less testing conditions, ran to just a similar level as on hurdling bow upped in grade, though he probably wasn't seen to best effect the way things unfolded, also nowhere near as battle hardened as most of those that beat him; soon steadied, travelled fluently, ridden from 2 out, one paced; still early days, he remains with potential. **Aircraft Carrier** without a tongue strap this time, faced a stiff task in this grade; always behind. **Home By The Lee** ran no sort of race upped in trip and grade and is better judged on previous form for the time being; raced off the pace, not always fluent, never landed a blow.

Ladbrokes Dublin Chase (Grade 1)

Pos	*Btn*	*Horse*	*Age*	*Wgt*	*Eq*	*Trainer*	*Jockey*	*SP*
1		CHACUN POUR SOI (FR)	8	11-10		W. P. Mullins, Ireland	P. Townend	6/5f
2	3¾	MIN (FR)	9	11-10		W. P. Mullins, Ireland	Robbie Power	7/4
3	24	ORNUA (IRE)	9	11-10		Henry de Bromhead, Ireland	D. Robinson	66/1
4	4	CASTLEGRACE PADDY (IRE)	9	11-10	(t)	P. A. Fahy, Ireland	B. J. Cooper	66/1
F		CILAOS EMERY (FR)	8	11-10	(h)	W. P. Mullins, Ireland	D. E. Mullins	4/1
F		DUC DES GENIEVRES (FR)	7	11-10	(t)	W. P. Mullins, Ireland	M. P. Walsh	16/1
pu		ORDINARY WORLD (IRE)	10	11-10		Henry de Bromhead, Ireland	Davy Russell	25/1

7 ran Race Time 4m 09.70 Closing Sectional (4.40f): 66.60s (97.0%) Winning Owner: Mrs S. Ricci

The latest renewal of the Dublin Chase might not have had the depth of December's Tingle Creek Chase, but it did offer up an intriguing clash between 2 of the very best 2m chasers in Ireland and it took a performance of outstanding merit to win it, Chacun Pour Soi producing a rating matched only by Cyrname this season to fend off his illustrious stablemate Min after the pair had engaged in a private duel from the third last. **Chacun Pour Soi** had looked something out of the ordinary when beating Defi du Seuil a Grade 1 at Punchestown as a novice chaser and duly confirmed that impression here, the manner in which he glided past a top-class rival in Min approaching the home turn marking him down as a chaser of the very highest order; chased leaders, jumped soundly in main, travelled well, upsides 3 out, jumped on next, ridden before last, kept going well; open to further progress, he looks sure to take plenty of beating if lining up in what promises to be a Champion Chase to savour at Cheltenham next month. **Min** was bidding to win this race for the third successive year but found a slightly younger, less exposed rival too good after 7 weeks off; close up, travelled well, jumped on fifth, joined 3 out, outjumped next and lost share of lead, ridden entering straight, kept on, pulled clear of rest; he's entered in both the Champion Chase and the Ryanair Chase at Cheltenham, though having twice come up short in the former against Altior, not to mention the likelihood of both Chacun Pour Soi and Defi du Seuil also lining up there, it's surely the Ryanair that will provide him with the best chance of gaining an as yet elusive Cheltenham Festival success. **Ornua** faced a stiff task in this company but hasn't gone on from reappearance in any case; led until not fluent fifth, lost place next, no threat from 4 out and merely plugged on for third run-in. **Castlegrace Paddy** goes well fresh and shaped a bit better than the distance beaten suggests after 9 months off, albeit without posing a threat to the principals; raced off the pace, some headway after 3 out, left in a place 2 out, weakened run-in. **Cilaos Emery** got no further than the first, losing his unbeaten record in this sphere. **Duc des Genievres** hasn't really kicked on as expected this season, in the process of being put in his place when departing late on; in touch, took closer order from 4 out, mistake 3 out, looked held in third when fell 2 out. **Ordinary World** ran no sort of race; soon detached, struggling from third, pulled up before fifth, possibly amiss.

ERSG Arkle Novice Chase (Grade 1)

Pos	Btn	Horse	Age	Wgt	Eq	Trainer	Jockey	SP
1		NOTEBOOK (GER)	7	11-10	(t)	Henry de Bromhead, Ireland	Rachael Blackmore	5/4f
2	¾	CASH BACK (FR)	8	11-10	(h)	W. P. Mullins, Ireland	D. E. Mullins	10/3
3	7	GALLANT JOHN JOE (IRE)	7	11-10	(s)	Oliver McKiernan, Ireland	B. Browne	25/1
4	12	MELON	8	11-10		W. P. Mullins, Ireland	P. Townend	4/1
5	1¾	ROYAL RENDEZVOUS (IRE)	8	11-10	(h)	W. P. Mullins, Ireland	M. P. Fogarty	14/1
6	57	BAPAUME (FR)	7	11-10	(t)	W. P. Mullins, Ireland	Robbie Power	9/2

6 ran Race Time 4m 14.00 Closing Sectional (4.40f): 65.4s (100.5%) Winning Owner: Gigginstown House Stud

A tremendous spectacle, Cash Back and Notebook jumping like old hands at the head of affairs and having the remainder burned off before 2 out, the latter pulling out a bit extra on the run-in to land his second Grade 1 of the season. **Notebook** the best seen out in this division this season, made it 4 from 4 over fences in tenacious fashion, jumping impeccably again and finding plenty to get the better of a protracted duel with the runner-up; pulled hard to start, tracked pace, jumped impeccably, edged ahead entering straight, dug deep under pressure; bordering on high-class now, he will head to Cheltenham as one of the Irish bankers. **Cash Back** lost nothing in defeat, improving another chunk in fact, lots to like about the way he made the high-class winner pull out all the stops; made running, jumped well in main, headed between last 2, rallied well, no extra only late on; deserves to have another crack at Notebook in the Cheltenham equivalent. **Gallant John Joe** retried in headgear, produced a career best—on just his second start over fences—to turn around form from last time with Melon; held up, pushed along 4 out, went third early in straight, kept on, no match for principals; sure to win races over fences. **Melon** wasn't in the same form as last time, not jumping with the same alacrity as the first 2 and readily left behind by that pair from 3 out; mid-division, slow sixth, left behind soon after 3 out, no further impression; will prove suited by 2½m in this sphere. **Royal Rendezvous** ran to a similar level to last time; waited with, blundered first, behind when hit 2 out, kept on, never a threat; probably needs dropping in class. **Bapaume** at the shortest trip he has tackled since finishing last of 8 in the Irish Champion Hurdle on this card 2 years ago, ran no sort of race; held up, plenty to do when mistake 3 out, beaten soon after, not persevered with once held.

PCI Irish Champion Hurdle (Grade 1)

Pos	Btn	Horse	Age	Wgt	Eq	Trainer	Jockey	SP
1		HONEYSUCKLE	6	11-3		Henry de Bromhead, Ireland	Rachael Blackmore	8/11f
2	½	DARVER STAR (IRE)	8	11-10	(t)	Gavin Patrick Cromwell, Ireland	Jonathan Moore	20/1
3	½	PETIT MOUCHOIR (FR)	9	11-10	(s)	Henry de Bromhead, Ireland	Davy Russell	9/1
4	3¾	SUPASUNDAE	10	11-10	(t)	Mrs J. Harrington, Ireland	Robbie Power	12/1
5	3¾	ARAMON (GER)	7	11-10		W. P. Mullins, Ireland	P. Townend	20/1
6	2¼	SHARJAH (FR)	7	11-10	(t)	W. P. Mullins, Ireland	Mr P. W. Mullins	2/1
7	11	MONSIEUR LECOQ (FR)	6	11-10		Mrs Jane Williams	Lizzie Kelly	25/1
8	12	SAGLAWY (FR)	6	11-10		W. P. Mullins, Ireland	M. P. Walsh	33/1
9	62	BALLYCAINES (IRE)	5	11-9		B. A. Murphy, Ireland	Sean Flanagan	100/1

9 ran Race Time 3m 50.10 Closing Sectional (5.40f): 74.60s (104.1%) Winning Owner: Kenneth Alexander

Not exactly a rich source of Champion Hurdle winners in recent years, Hurricane Fly in 2013 the last one to complete the double, and this latest renewal wasn't quite so informative as it promised to be, the withdrawal of last year's Supreme winner Klassical Dream and a below-par effort from Sharjah taking some of the gloss off the form, Honeysuckle getting the job done but not before giving her growing legion of supporters a few anxious moments, one stepping out of novice company pushing her all the way the line; the pace was little better than fair, a point borne out by the fact that the rank outsider, Ballycaines, was still with the main body of the field 3 out. **Honeysuckle** back down in trip and on a left-handed track for the first time under Rules, extended her winning sequence with a performance that caused few ripples in the Champion Hurdle market, no more than workmanlike on the day, class getting her through; tracked pace, travelled well, went on early in straight, headed when awkward last, found extra; more will be required at Cheltenham—assuming, of course, that she takes her chance in the Champion Hurdle rather than the David Nicholson—but it is entirely possible that the best is yet to come. **Darver Star** tackling open Grade 1 company for the first time, showed much improved form and paid a handsome compliment to Envoi Allen into the bargain; chased leaders, ridden entering straight, closed all the way to the line; remains to be seen if able to back this up. **Petit Mouchoir** confirmed that he is back to his very best and briefly looked like he was going to win for the first time over hurdles since taking this contest in 2017; made running, headed approaching last, led again briefly run-in, no extra only dying strides. **Supasundae** a previous winner of this race (runner-up to Apple's Jade last year), shaped as if retaining all ability on his first start for 9 months; mid-division, pushed along before 3 out, kept on, never landed a blow. **Aramon** ran much better than last time without carrying any sort of win threat, not up to this grade; dropped out, took closer order before 2 out, kept on, never landed a blow. **Sharjah** can have a line put through this run, clearly not 100% on the day; chased leaders, not always fluent, ridden 2 out, soon done with; type to bounce back quickly and won't be one to dismiss lightly if lining up at Cheltenham. **Monsieur Lecoq** has yet to prove he belongs at this level in 2 tries of late; mid-division, ridden before 2 out, beaten when mistake last. **Saglawy** faced a stiff task in this grade but is best not judged on this run; patiently ridden, still plenty to do but yet to be asked for effort when chance-ending mistake 2 out, not recover. **Ballycaines** fit from the Flat, was hopelessly out of depth on his first start over jumps since joining this yard; held up, lost touch soon after 3 out.

LEOPARDSTOWN Sunday February 2

SOFT

Chanelle Pharma Novice Hurdle (Brave Inca) (Grade 1)

Pos	Btn	Horse	Age	Wgt	Eq	Trainer	Jockey	SP
1		ASTERION FORLONGE (FR)	6	11-10		W. P. Mullins, Ireland	D. E. Mullins	4/1
2	9½	EASYWORK (FR)	6	11-10	(h)	Gordon Elliott, Ireland	J. W. Kennedy	5/4f
3	4	MT LEINSTER (IRE)	6	11-10	(h)	W. P. Mullins, Ireland	P. Townend	5/2
4	4	CONFLATED (IRE)	6	11-10		Gordon Elliott, Ireland	Davy Russell	12/1
5	71	JASON THE MILITANT (IRE)	6	11-10		Henry de Bromhead, Ireland	Rachael Blackmore	20/1
6	58	THE LITTLE YANK (IRE)	5	11-9		John Patrick Ryan, Ireland	Liam Quinlan	100/1
pu		BLUE SARI (FR)	5	11-9		W. P. Mullins, Ireland	M. P. Walsh	13/2

7 ran Race Time 3m 59.00 Closing Sectional (5.40f): 82.6s (97.7%) Winning Owner: Mrs J. Donnelly

Often the strongest pre-Cheltenham novice hurdle either side of the Irish Sea, as in both years since the distance was reduced to 2m the winner has gone on to follow up comfortably at Cheltenham—Samcro in the Ballymore and Klassical Dream in the Supreme—while a further twice last decade a Mullins-trained winner went on to land the Supreme, and this latest renewal looks really strong form, run at an unrelenting gallop, the winner clearing away impressively from a pair of very useful novices to put himself atop the pile of likely runners in the Festival opener. **Asterion Forlonge** might have made his debut over hurdles only after the turn of the year but already looks one of the very brightest novices around—Envoi Allen included—in the way he dismantled a pair who'd looked really good prospects themselves; he disputed the lead at a really strong clip with Easywork, wasn't fluent at the third (and tended to jump right again) yet what he did off the home turn, quickly drawing clear, was most impressive, still looking raw but staying on well as he was driven out; unbeaten in a point, a bumper and now 2 hurdle starts, he's most exciting and this level of form entitles him to be favourite for the Supreme over the same owner's Shishkin as things stand. **Easywork** might have lost his unbeaten record over hurdles but there'll be other days for him, worth remembering his strength in the market, while his future seemingly lies back over further after this defeat, admittedly at the hands of a potential top-notcher; disputed lead, left behind by winner early in straight, awkward last, one paced; we haven't yet seen the best of him. **Mt Leinster** seemingly the yard's first string, is not there yet with his jumping after all, seeming to be getting a good tow into the race from the first pair before a particularly bad error 2 out (not his first) appeared to knock the stuffing out of him, unable to pick up in the straight; he remains capable of better and has the engine to go close in other Grade 1 events in the spring should his jumping stand up better. **Conflated** without usual hood, has form behind some of the best novices around over further than this but was taken off his feet faced with a very well-run 2m; soon behind, uncomfortable with pace, still long way back when not fluent 2 out, stayed on gradually; he'll benefit from the return to 2½m+ and could be one for the Martin Pipe at Cheltenham, mark depending. **Jason The Militant** was biting off more than he could chew in this company; chased leaders, lost ground fifth, took 2 out alongside Conflated but weakened and was eased soon after. **The Little Yank** was out of his depth; raced off the pace, not fluent first, labouring fifth, beaten long way out. **Blue Sari** alarmingly weak in the market in the minutes before the off, shaped as if having a major issue for the second start in a row; mid-field, ridden after 3 out, folded as if amiss and pulled up before next; it's hard to know what to make of him at present.

Flogas Novice Chase (Scalp) (Grade 1)

Pos	Btn	Horse	Age	Wgt	Eq	Trainer	Jockey	SP
1		FAUGHEEN (IRE)	12	11-10		W. P. Mullins, Ireland	P. Townend	13/8jf
2	½	EASY GAME (FR)	6	11-10		W. P. Mullins, Ireland	Robbie Power	5/1
3	6	TORNADO FLYER (IRE)	7	11-10		W. P. Mullins, Ireland	D. E. Mullins	11/1
4	4¾	CASTLEBAWN WEST (IRE)	7	11-10	(h)	W. P. Mullins, Ireland	M. P. Fogarty	14/1
5	65	MYTH BUSTER (IRE)	7	11-10		Henry de Bromhead, Ireland	Keith Donoghue	50/1
F		BATTLEOVERDOYEN (IRE)	7	11-10	(t)	Gordon Elliott, Ireland	Davy Russell	13/8jf
ur		DOMMAGE POUR TOI (FR)	7	11-10		Henry de Bromhead, Ireland	Rachael Blackmore	40/1

7 ran Race Time 5m 34.20 Closing Sectional (4.40f): 68.90s (101.6%) Winning Owner: Mrs S. Ricci

A heart-warming victory for the evergreen veteran Faugheen, though the fact Willie Mullins also saddled the next 3 home is indicative of the strength in depth he currently possesses in the novice chase division and that is arguably the most important thing to take from the race when looking ahead to the big Spring festivals; the pace wasn't a bad one, with the front-running Battleoverdoyen possibly paying the price for taking on Faugheen from the off. **Faugheen** remains the best novice chaser seen out so far in 2019/20, though this latest Grade 1 success doesn't represent so strong form as his Limerick win, whilst the fact his jumping hasn't looked assured now on 2 of his 3 starts over fences (also often clumsy over hurdles) is worth bearing in mind should he turn up at prohibitive odds at the Cheltenham Festival; never far away, not always fluent, went on between 3 out and

2 out, hit last 2, dug deep under pressure. **Easy Game** is clearly a much better chaser than hurdler (his chasing debut defeat of stable-companion Allaho reads even better now) and looks well up to winning in Grade 1 company before the season is out; waited with, still plenty to do entering back straight, crept closer from 4 out, challenged home turn, just failed. **Tornado Flyer** wasted no time getting back on track, losing little in defeat against 2 rivals a bit higher up the Mullins pecking order; mid-division, blundered 3 out (jumped okay otherwise), kept on from home turn. **Castlebawn West** faced a stiff task in this grade and ran perfectly well; mid-division, in contention home turn, brushed aside soon after (left in fourth last); remains open to improvement with his sights lowered slightly. **Myth Buster** needs to brush up his jumping but remains open to improvement in this sphere, his third here in December looking strong form; held up, blundered ninth, not fluent again next, not recover. **Battleoverdoyen** lost his unbeaten record over fences, the decision to take on market rival Faugheen from the off seeming to backfire, better judged on that earlier form as a result; made running, headed approaching 2 out, weakening in fourth when fell last (fluent until then). **Dommage Pour Toi** faced a stiff task back over fences and failed to complete; held up, still behind when unseated rider 3 out.

Paddy Power Irish Gold Cup Chase (Grade 1)

Pos	*Btn*	*Horse*	*Age*	*Wgt*	*Eq*	*Trainer*	*Jockey*	*SP*
1		DELTA WORK (FR)	7	11-10	(h+t)	Gordon Elliott, Ireland	J. W. Kennedy	5/2
2	1½	KEMBOY (FR)	8	11-10		W. P. Mullins, Ireland	P. Townend	5/4f
3	3¼	PRESENTING PERCY	9	11-10	(t)	Patrick G. Kelly, Ireland	Davy Russell	10/3
4	4¾	JETT (IRE)	9	11-10	(s)	Mrs J. Harrington, Ireland	Robbie Power	40/1
5	4	LA BAGUE AU ROI (FR)	9	11-3		Warren Greatrex	M. P. Walsh	14/1
6	47	BELLSHILL (IRE)	10	11-10	(t)	W. P. Mullins, Ireland	Mr P. W. Mullins	14/1
7	34	CADMIUM (FR)	8	11-10		W. P. Mullins, Ireland	D. E. Mullins	33/1
8	nk	ANIBALE FLY (FR)	10	11-10	(t)	A. J. Martin, Ireland	Barry Geraghty	25/1

8 ran Race Time 6m 25.50 Closing Sectional (4.40f): 70.60s (100.1%) Winning Owner: Gigginstown House Stud

Al Boum Photo and Monalee were just about the only leading Irish stayers missing from what was a cracking renewal of the Irish Gold Cup and, with the pace a sound one, the cream duly rose to the top as the 3 market principals fought things out, an assured round of jumping by Delta Work proving decisive as he confirmed his Savills Chase superiority over Kemboy. **Delta Work** stepped up again to follow up his Savills Chase win and, although a few rivals might have posted higher ratings in their recent past, this reliable gelding appeals as one of the most solid candidates in what looks an open year for the Cheltenham Gold Cup itself, particularly as further improvement cannot be ruled out (now 6 wins from 8 starts in this sphere); waited with, jumped accurately (his Down Royal display increasingly looks a blip), crept closer from halfway, stayed on to lead last, held on gamely. **Kemboy** stepped up on his recent run without matching the form of his Punchestown Gold Cup win (which remains the strongest in this division), some slipshod jumping in the final third of the race ultimately proving costly against an up-and-coming rival; never far away, typically travelled strongly, clouted twelfth, not fluent next, led 2 out, headed last, rallied. **Presenting Percy** is clearly still a top-class performer but had no apparent excuses this time, which rather tempers enthusiasm for his Cheltenham Gold Cup prospects; waited with, crept closer from early final circuit, every chance 2 out, kept on. **Jett** is holding his form well this winter, minor prize money the best he can hope for at this exalted level; mid-division, jumped on 4 out, headed 2 out (mistake there), left behind from home turn. **La Bague Au Roi** had far more miles on the clock than the other leading novices of 2018/19 so it isn't the biggest surprise she's failed to progress like many of those rivals this winter, needing no excuses in the face of a stiff task back up in trip here; led until third, remained prominent, readily outpaced from home turn. **Bellshill** has now flopped on all 4 starts since winning the 2019 edition of this race (which was run on controversial ground), turning in a lacklustre display in a first-time tongue strap here; soon behind, mistake eighth, never really going well after, tailed off. **Cadmium** shaped as if retaining ability upped in trip and shouldn't be written off once his sights are lowered a bit, with another tilt at the Topham Chase presumably on the cards this Spring; went with zest, led from third, headed 4 out, dropped away from next. **Anibale Fly** is possibly having his campaign geared towards the Grand National (fourth in 2018 and fifth in 2019) rather than the Cheltenham Gold Cup (placed last 2 years) this time around but, even so, he seems to be struggling for form at present; mid-division, off the bridle long way out, tailed off 4 out.

CHELTENHAM Tuesday March 10

SOFT

Sky Bet Supreme Novices' Hurdle (Grade 1) (1)

Pos	Btn	Horse	Age	Wgt	Eq	Trainer	Jockey	SP
1		SHISHKIN (IRE)	6	11-7		Nicky Henderson	Nico de Boinville	6/1
2	hd	ABACADABRAS (FR)	6	11-7		Gordon Elliott, Ireland	Davy Russell	11/4
3	11	CHANTRY HOUSE (IRE)	6	11-7		Nicky Henderson	Barry Geraghty	15/2
4	2¾	ASTERION FORLONGE (FR)	6	11-7		W. P. Mullins, Ireland	P. Townend	9/4f
5	1½	ALLART (IRE)	6	11-7		Nicky Henderson	James Bowen	33/1
6	8	EDWARDSTONE	6	11-7		Alan King	Tom Cannon	25/1
7	8	HEAVEN HELP US (IRE)	6	11-0		Paul Hennessy, Ireland	D. E. Mullins	100/1
8	6½	WHATSNOTOKNOW (IRE)	5	11-7	(t)	M. F. Morris, Ireland	Philip Enright	100/1
9	11	SOVIET PIMPERNEL (IRE)	5	11-7		Peter Fahey, Ireland	K. C. Sexton	50/1
10	9½	HOLLOW SOUND (IRE)	5	11-7		Luke Comer, Ireland	Mr D. T. Kelly	150/1
11	2¾	FIDDLERONTHEROOF (IRE)	6	11-7		Colin Tizzard	Robbie Power	6/1
12	19	BERKSHIRE ROYAL	5	11-7		W. P. Mullins, Ireland	Dave Crosse	100/1
F		ELIXIR D'AINAY (FR)	6	11-7		W. P. Mullins, Ireland	M. P. Walsh	16/1
bd		CAPTAIN GUINNESS (IRE)	5	11-7		Henry de Bromhead, Ireland	Rachael Blackmore	14/1
pu		MARIO DE PAIL (FR)	5	11-7		Sam Thomas	Sam Twiston-Davies	100/1

15 ran Race Time 4m 08.00 Closing Sectional (4.1f): 61.0s (101.6%) Winning Owner: Mrs J Donnelly

For the third year running the Cheltenham Festival started on soft ground, almost a thing of the past prior to 2018, the conditions bordering on heavy and bringing stamina into play, even in a race not run at a flat-out gallop; the field for the Supreme looked a representative one, save for the notable absence of last season's Champion Bumper winner Envoi Allen, running in the Baring Bingham instead, the form of the pair that finished clear looking well up to scratch for an average renewal, though clearly others might have had a hand in the finish but for some serious interference 2 out, the first 2 doing well to avoid being more significantly hampered themselves; the field was a good one on looks on the whole and plenty make appeal as potential chasers, not least the winner. **Shishkin** had looked an excellent prospect in winning his 2 completed starts over hurdles and duly built on that with a gutsy performance, belying a market drift and suited by the test of stamina back down in trip; in touch, mistake third, hampered soon after, switched before 3 out, ridden after, hampered 2 out, stayed on straight, challenged last, stayed on to lead final 50 yds; he's very much a chaser on looks and seems set to embark on a career over fences in the autumn, an exciting prospect whatever route is taken with him. **Abacadabras** beaten only by Envoi

Allen over hurdles previously, was strong in the betting and ran a cracker, looking much more the finished article than he had in the Champion Bumper last season, just denied by a slightly stronger stayer having tanked his way through the race; held up, travelled well, good progress 3 out, hampered next, led on bridle approaching last, joined there, ridden run-in, headed final 50 yds, stuck to task; he looks a chaser, though his trainer suggested afterwards that he would be aimed at the Champion Hurdle next season, plenty about the way he did things to encourage that option. **Chantry House** was easy to back but ran well upped in grade, for all he lost his unbeaten record, a lot to like about what he has done this season; handy, travelled well, shaken up after 2 out, held when hampered last, stayed on; he's an exciting chasing prospect for 2020/21, no surprise if he's back here a leading Arkle contender in 12 months. **Asterion Forlonge** strong in the betting, couldn't get away with jumping markedly right this time and lost his unbeaten record, doing well to hold on to fourth in the circumstances; led, travelled well, ridden home turn, headed soon after, no extra; he'll presumably go to Punchestown, where the track ought to suit him a lot better. **Allart** ran about as well as could have been expected upped in grade, giving his stable 3 of the first 5 home, like the other pair a good prospect for fences next season, bred to stay further than 2m as well, so still with untapped potential; held up, took keen hold, mistake fourth, headway 3 out, ridden straight, not quicken last. **Edwardstone** without the hood this time, seemed likely to be suited by the way the race developed, but failed to show his best, not seeing things out fully on this different type of track; in rear, took keen hold, not fluent first, some headway 3 out, no extra approaching last; he could well do a fair bit better if sent to Aintree for the Top Novices', and his physique and demeanour both suggest a smart chasing prospect for next season. **Heaven Help Us** had plenty on in this company, on ground softer than she'd mostly raced, though in the event she didn't get to show what she could do, easy to put a line through this run; waited with, effort before 3 out, headway when hampered there, also badly hampered next, not recover. **Whatsnotoknow** had taken 4 goes to win a maiden and had shown nothing to suggest he could make an impact at this level; handy, shaken up before 2 out, weakened home turn. **Soviet Pimpernel** has had a productive season, but was biting off more than he could chew in this company; chased leaders, took keen hold, lost place before 3 out. **Hollow Sound** looked out of place beforehand and unsurprisingly proved so in the race itself; raced off the pace, labouring fifth, tailed off. **Fiddlerontheroof** with some strong form to his name, looked to have plenty going for him, not least the testing conditions, and proved the major disappointment of the race, in trouble a long way out; chased leaders, pushed along fifth, labouring after next; his overall profile suggests he will bounce back sooner rather than later. **Berkshire Royal** useful on the Flat, stays 12.5f, was asked an awful lot after nearly 18 months off on his hurdling debut/first outing since leaving Andrew Balding for 130,000 gns, racing on very testing ground having run on nothing worse than good to soft on the Flat; dropped out, labouring fifth, tailed off next; his Flat form and his excellent trainer offer clear hope that he will do significantly better, though this as a start was unpromising. **Elixir d'Ainay** was in the process of running well when he was taken out of the race, effectively knocked over by the errant favourite; close up, hampered 3 out, yet to be asked for effort when hampered and fell next; he looks the part for chasing. **Captain Guinness** was shaping well, given his want of experience, and set to run better again when he was taken out of the race through no fault of his own; waited with, took keen hold, going well when hampered 3 out, brought down next. **Mario de Pail** had loads to find to make an impact in this company and just wasn't near up to the task; raced off the pace, ridden after fifth, tailed off 3 out, pulled up straight.

Racing Post Arkle Challenge Trophy Novices' Chase (Grade 1) (1)

Pos	Btn	Horse	Age	Wgt	Eq	Trainer	Jockey	SP
1		PUT THE KETTLE ON (IRE)	6	10-11		Henry de Bromhead, Ireland	Aidan Coleman	16/1
2	1½	FAKIR D'OUDAIRIES (FR)	5	11-4		Joseph Patrick O'Brien, Ireland	M. P. Walsh	3/1
3	18	ROUGE VIF (FR)	6	11-4	(t)	Harry Whittington	Gavin Sheehan	9/1
4	hd	GLOBAL CITIZEN (IRE)	8	11-4	(t)	Ben Pauling	David Bass	33/1
5	2½	AL DANCER (FR)	7	11-4		Nigel Twiston-Davies	Sam Twiston-Davies	16/1
6	5	NOTEBOOK (GER)	7	11-4	(t)	Henry de Bromhead, Ireland	Rachael Blackmore	5/2f
F		MAIRE BANRIGH	8	10-11	(t)	Dan Skelton	Harry Skelton	16/1
F		CASH BACK (FR)	8	11-4	(h)	W. P. Mullins, Ireland	P. Townend	6/1
F		ESPRIT DU LARGE (FR)	6	11-4		Evan Williams	Adam Wedge	12/1
ur		BREWIN'UPASTORM (IRE)	7	11-4		Olly Murphy	Richard Johnson	6/1
pu		OUR MERLIN	8	11-4		Robert Walford	Stan Sheppard	100/1

11 ran Race Time 4m 08.40 Closing Sectional (3.75f): 60.2s (97.3%) Winning Owner: One For Luck Racing Syndicate

A deep field assembled for the Arkle, winners of the 3 pre-Cheltenham Grade 1 novice chases at this trip lining up, together with the runners-up from the 2 of those held in Ireland—one of those horses himself already a Grade 1 winner over further—along with a trio of Grade 2 winners plus a further 2 unbeaten chasers; in the event the race was a bit of an anti-climax, Notebook and Cash Back charging the tape at the first attempt, both of them taking a little while to pull up and get back to the start before not running their race, plenty of incident at the fourth last and only a pair ending up giving their running, the result of greater relevance in historical rather than form terms—the winner the first mare to land this in 40 years; that the first 2 are both fully proven over 2½m was probably an advantage given how things panned out, the pace unsurprisingly a good one from the outset, even if those that remained were still closely bunched after 3 out. **Put The Kettle On** had gained valuable course experience when winning in November, though even that success wasn't definitive proof that the Arkle would be her Festival target, having the option of the Marsh (stays 2½m) as well as the novice handicap from a mark of 144, her trainer rewarded in picking the right race and, while she might emerge as only the fourth best mare to have run on the day, she cemented her place in Festival history in becoming the first of her sex to land this prize since Anaglogs Daughter some 40 years earlier; lean and slightly sweaty beforehand, she travelled well and jumped superbly pressing the leader, led on the bridle 3 out, got a bit of a break courtesy of the runner-up's mistake at the next before she idled somewhat on the run-in; her jumping will continue to stand her in good stead and, having missed the winter months, could well have other spring festivals on her agenda. **Fakir d'Oudairies** might have already been a Grade 1 winner over fences but still took his form up another notch after 11 weeks off, not least as his weight-for-age allowance had eroded completely, running another cracker at this meeting for a young horse, and he might well have won had he avoided the errors like the winner did; sweating beforehand, he reached for the second but travelled better than most chasing the leaders, and even after being short of room after 5 out and hitting the next he moved up into second going well after 3 out, holding every chance when blundering 2 out and rallying on the run-in but held final 100 yds, a long way clear of the remainder; he's not an immature horse but is still entitled to improve a little further through the spring and into next season. **Rouge Vif** emerged best of the home-trained contingent despite running some way below the form of his Warwick win, also beaten even further by the winner than he had been here in November; racing in mid-field, he stood off at the sixth, got himself into contention briefly after 3 out but couldn't quicken turning for home, keeping on again on the run-in to take a remote third in the dying strides. **Global Citizen** another coming here without a run in the calendar year, shaped better than the distance beaten suggests, one of the worst affected by the standing start and also suffering interference at the top of the hill before working his way into contention; slowly into stride, held up, not settle fully, steadied into sixth and generally not that fluent back straight, badly hampered 4 out, good progress out wide approaching next, threatened briefly before home turn, no extra latter stages, lost third on line. **Al Dancer** wasn't beaten far by Put The Kettle On here in November but has since shown that he falls shy of the top novices, his jumping put under a bit of pressure in this environment; mid-division, not always fluent, hampered 4 out, not quicken next. **Notebook** who stood out on form, previously unbeaten over fences including a pair of top-level successes, got to the start okay this time but was revved up once there, he and Cash Back charging the tape at the first attempted start, and he just didn't run his race, clear from starting off down the hill that his rider wasn't particularly happy with him; chased leaders, took keen hold, shaken up after 4 out, had to really fight for room after next, held when jumped right 2 out, no extra; hopefully, he'll settle down a bit in time and there's every chance physically that he'll be even better next season. **Maire Banrigh** the pick of the paddock—a strapping mare—and previously unbeaten over fences, though in much lesser company, seemed to have warmed into a good rhythm when getting the final ditch all wrong; raced along inside, tracked pace, not fluent second, yet to be asked for effort when fell 4 out; she suffered an injury, though not believed to be life threatening. **Cash Back** second to Notebook in the Irish equivalent, just like that one failed to run his race at all, the pair of them having charged the tape at the first attempt; led, not always fluent (and a bit to his right at times), took strong hold, headed 3 out, weakening when shuffled back soon after, behind when fell 2 out. **Esprit du Large** off the track since winning the Henry VIII 3 months earlier, got involved from the second half of the field and might have been in the mix for a place but for departing, though would have run a fair way below his Sandown form; soon steadied, crept closer 5 out, mistake next, chased leaders 3 out, not quicken entering straight, held in fifth when fell heavily 2 out. **Brewin'upastorm** who'd been restricted to just 2 previous chase starts, was caught out by his inexperience, still off the pace when ploughing through 4 out and giving Johnson no chance of staying aboard, having already pecked at the sixth after he was slowly into stride; he remains open to improvement, his Taunton defeat of Southfield Stone looking better now than it did at the time. **Our Merlin** after just one previous run over fences, predictably struggled in this grade after 9 weeks off, losing touch when hampered slightly in the melee 4 out.

Unibet Champion Hurdle Challenge Trophy (Grade 1) (1)

Pos	*Btn*	*Horse*	*Age*	*Wgt*	*Eq*	*Trainer*	*Jockey*	*SP*
1		EPATANTE (FR)	6	11-3		Nicky Henderson	Barry Geraghty	2/1f
2	3	SHARJAH (FR)	7	11-10	(t)	W. P. Mullins, Ireland	Mr P. W. Mullins	16/1
3	3¾	DARVER STAR (IRE)	8	11-10	(t)	Gavin Patrick Cromwell, Ireland	Jonathan Moore	17/2
4	2¾	CILAOS EMERY (FR)	8	11-10	(h)	W. P. Mullins, Ireland	P. Townend	7/1
5	2	PETIT MOUCHOIR (FR)	9	11-10	(s)	Henry de Bromhead, Ireland	Rachael Blackmore	25/1
6	½	SILVER STREAK (IRE)	7	11-10		Evan Williams	Adam Wedge	20/1

7	2½	SUPASUNDAE	10	11-10	(t)	Mrs J. Harrington, Ireland	Robbie Power	9/1
8	1½	BALLYANDY	9	11-10		Nigel Twiston-Davies	Sam Twiston-Davies	20/1
9	3	PENTLAND HILLS (IRE)	5	11-10		Nicky Henderson	Nico de Boinville	9/1
10	1	DARASSO (FR)	7	11-10		Joseph Patrick O'Brien, Ireland	M. P. Walsh	40/1
11	6	FUSIL RAFFLES (FR)	5	11-10		Nicky Henderson	Daryl Jacob	20/1
12	2¾	GUMBALL (FR)	6	11-10	(h)	Philip Hobbs	Aidan Coleman	100/1
13	1¼	CALL ME LORD (FR)	7	11-10		Nicky Henderson	James Bowen	10/1
14	1¼	LE PATRIOTE (FR)	8	11-10	(b)	Dr Richard Newland	Charlie Hammond	100/1
15	24	COEUR SUBLIME (IRE)	5	11-10	(t)	Gordon Elliott, Ireland	Davy Russell	12/1
pu		CORNERSTONE LAD	6	11-10		Micky Hammond	Henry Brooke	33/1
pu		NOT SO SLEEPY	8	11-10	(t)	Hughie Morrison	Jonathan Burke	33/1

17 ran Race Time 4m 07.60 Closing Sectional (4.1f): 59s (104.9%) Winning Owner: Mr John P. McManus

The largest field for the Champion Hurdle since 23 went to post in 2009, though quantity wasn't matched with quality, most having best form which was some way short of the standard usually required, the bare form of Epatante's win, with the mares allowance, earning a rating from Timeform as low as any winner this century, though she was value for a bit more than the winning margin and the runner-up produced an effort marginally better than Sublimity and Hors La Loi III achieved in winning the race; there was quite a notable list of absentees that might have made an impact, including the first 2 in the Mares' Hurdle, last season's Champion Bumper winner Envoi Allen, the sidelined dual Champion Buveur d'Air, the very smart mare Verdana Blue, the Betfair Hurdle winner Pic d'Orhy and even the first 2 in the Supreme, not to mention the pick of a strong crop of juveniles, while the winner herself was a rumoured doubt for the race the previous week, reported to have coughed, Benie des Dieux, who would have needed to be supplemented, briefly an improbable favourite ante-post; for the third time on the afternoon, the race began from a standing start after the starter hadn't been happy with the field lining up, such an outcome entirely predictable and unsatisfactory, a review of starting procedures surely overdue, including the question of whether the starters themselves are contributing to the problem, the current system of the starters effectively marking their own homework, by deciding whether any riders were at fault, not allowing for that possibility. **Epatante** looked the one to beat on her form in winning the Christmas Hurdle and justified strong support in following up, coping well with more of a test of stamina than for either of her races earlier in the season, banishing ghosts from her poor performance when favourite for the Dawn Run in 2019; in touch, travelled well, not fluent 3 out, tracked pace home turn, jumped on last, ridden run-in, kept on well, won readily; she was a class better than an ordinary field, not required to improve much on what she did last time, though she clearly has more to offer, a clash with Envoi Allen at Punchestown, say, likely to challenge her more than this race did. **Sharjah** duly put his poor showing at Leopardstown last time behind him, making his move after the winner, but not a threat to her after he went second; dropped out, travelled well, good progress approaching last, went second run-in, ran on, no impression on winner. **Darver Star** reached a place at Grade 1 level for the third start running, progressing a bit further, though with no excuses; chased leaders, travelled well, led approaching last, headed there, not quicken; he's developed into a very smart hurdler, though he probably won't be easy to place to actually win at this level. **Cilaos Emery** had been supplemented for this after his win at Gowran and performed with credit in a much stronger race, though never looking much like winning; held up, travelled well, not fluent fifth and pushed along briefly, headway next, shaken up 2 out, ridden straight, kept on, never landed a blow; he'd looked a bright chasing prospect earlier in the winter and surely a return to fences will be on the agenda into the spring. **Petit Mouchoir** third in the 2017 Champion Hurdle, ran about as well as could be expected, behind the runner-up and the third on his last 2 starts after all; led, clear briefly fifth, headed before last, one paced. **Silver Streak** third in last season's running, ran to a similar sort of level, his jumping rather hindering his chance, though perhaps a place better was all he might have managed; held up, mistake third, headway when not fluent fifth, not fluent again next, ridden after, plugged on straight, never landed a blow. **Supasundae** with a win in the 2017 Coral Cup and a second in the 2018 Stayers', couldn't enhance his Festival record, not finishing his race nearly so well as might have been expected; mid-division, pushed along 3 out, chased leaders straight, no extra last. **Ballyandy** wasn't disgraced, though couldn't add to a good Festival record, the form of his win last time and his effort in the International rather shown up in this, his third to the winner at Kempton the pick of his form this winter; handy, travelled well, not fluent 2 out, outpaced home turn. **Pentland Hills** who'd had a breathing operation since Haydock, was easy to back on the day and failed to meet expectations, the form of his 2 runs this season taking a knock in this race anyway, though he wasn't subjected to a hard race once it was clear he wasn't going to get involved; held up, effort briefly 3 out, not knocked about, never on terms; it's possible he may yet do better, though he now has questions to answer. **Darasso** was flying too high in this grade; slowly into stride, raced off the pace, effort after fifth, made little impression. **Fusil Raffles** disappointed for the second start running, having gone off joint favourite with the winner at Kempton, perhaps just no substance to his form for this sort of task; raced off the pace, not settle fully, labouring after fifth. **Gumball** was out of his depth; in touch, not settle fully, mistake fifth, weakened after next. **Call Me Lord** was well held, seeming unsettled by a mistake before halfway, the form of his win in the International hardly enhanced in this anyway; waited with, mistake fourth, labouring soon after. **Le Patriote** quickly back over hurdles, with blinkers replacing cheekpieces, was flying too high in this grade, though the way he moved into the race down the hill promised quite a bit more than he finally delivered, whether his attitude will allow him to capitalise on it in a more realistic race open to doubt; slowly into stride, held up, travelled well, good progress 3 out, ridden after next, soon done with, looked half-hearted. **Coeur Sublime** who'd had a breathing operation since running below form at Christmas, was well held in first-time tongue strap; mid-division, pushed along before 2 out, soon done with. **Cornerstone Lad** had plenty on in this company, but went as if amiss even so; close up, mistake fifth, ridden after, hung left, lost place soon after, pulled up next. **Not So Sleepy** had plenty on in this company, but for the second start running his chance was compromised by a false start, unable to make the most of his assets from a standing start; handy, not settle fully, mistake third, weakened 3 out, pulled up before last.

CHELTENHAM Wednesday March 11

SOFT,

Ballymore Novices' Hurdle (Baring Bingham) (Grade 1) (1)

Pos	*Btn*	*Horse*	*Age*	*Wgt*	*Eq*	*Trainer*	*Jockey*	*SP*
1		ENVOI ALLEN (FR)	6	11-7		Gordon Elliott, Ireland	Davy Russell	4/7f
2	4¼	EASYWORK (FR)	6	11-7	(h)	Gordon Elliott, Ireland	Rachael Blackmore	12/1
3	3¾	THE BIG GETAWAY (IRE)	6	11-7		W. P. Mullins, Ireland	P. Townend	9/1

4	6½	THE BIG BREAKAWAY (IRE)	5	11-7		Colin Tizzard	Robbie Power	8/1
5	8½	MOSSY FEN (IRE)	5	11-7		Nigel Twiston-Davies	Sam Twiston-Davies	33/1
6	4	SHAN BLUE (IRE)	6	11-7		Dan Skelton	Harry Skelton	100/1
7	3¼	SPORTING JOHN (IRE)	5	11-7		Philip Hobbs	Barry Geraghty	5/1
8	1	LONGHOUSE POET (IRE)	6	11-7	(t)	Martin Brassil, Ireland	M. P. Walsh	14/1
9	8	DECOR IRLANDAIS (FR)	7	11-7		Noel C. Kelly, Ireland	Mr N. McParlan	66/1
10	17	SHAKEM UP'ARRY (IRE)	6	11-7		Ben Pauling	Daryl Jacob	66/1
pu		GETAWAY FRED (IRE)	6	11-7		Colin Tizzard	Harry Cobden	100/1
pu		SON OF CAMAS (FR)	5	11-7		Nicky Henderson	Nico de Boinville	50/1

12 ran Race Time 5m 19.90 Closing Sectional (4.10f): 61.4s (101.7%) Winning Owner: Cheveley Park Stud

Envoi Allen, successful in a strong Champion Bumper last season, would have been a warm order whichever race he had contested at this Festival, with the Supreme and even the Champion Hurdle also under consideration, and he didn't have to improve much to land a third successive Grade 1 novice, particularly with his main rival on form running no sort of race, but there was still a lot to like about his performance, notably his slick hurdling and the way in which he picked up in the straight, his performance well up to standard for the race, the placed pair acquitting themselves well too, the home team not really at the races. **Envoi Allen** has made up into an imposing type, really filling the eye beforehand, and his performance was everything his record promised, the way in which he closed down the pair that had dominated and then went away from them with such authority a clear sign of a top-class prospect; mid-field, jumped well, took keen hold, chased leaders entering straight, headway to lead before last, in command soon after, impressive; so far as the rest of this season goes, he would be a really interesting contender for an open Grade 1, whether he stays hurdling or goes chasing next season, sure to continue to be very hard to beat. **Easywork** back up in trip, ran his best race yet, doing well considering his early keenness, sticking to his task admirably; prominent, not settle fully, shaken up 2 out, every chance approaching last, kept on, no match for winner; he's a less obvious chasing type than most of these on physique. **The Big Getaway** ran really well upped in grade, a lot to like about his performance for the future, like so many of this field a chaser in the making; close up, travelled well, led before fourth, pressed on seventh, headed approaching last, one paced. **The Big Breakaway** wasn't able to land a blow, but this was a big step up in grade and he shaped with plenty of encouragement, back on testing ground, sticking to his task well; waited with, outpaced after seventh, plugged on straight; he remains an exciting prospect, with chasing next season very much in mind. **Mossy Fen** ran about as well as could be expected in this company, being kept to this sort of trip probably not in his favour; in touch, pushed along before 3 out, outpaced next; he's shown himself a useful novice over hurdles, but he ought really to come into his own as a staying novice chaser next season. **Shan Blue** had plenty to find to figure in this company and just was not good enough; held up, shaken up before 3 out, mistake 2 out, made no impression; he should make at least as good a chaser, judged on looks. **Sporting John** was the disappointment of the race, looking the main threat on form to the favourite and impressing with the way he went through his races in lesser company, just not travelling from a long way out, a harbinger of the poor showing of stable-companion Defi du Seuil later in the afternoon; mid-division, took keen hold, labouring after halfway, left behind 3 out, finished distressed; hopefully, this will just be a blip in his progress. **Longhouse Poet** in his third successive Grade 1 novice, needed to improve again to have any prospect of getting involved and wasn't able to do so; in touch, not always fluent, labouring before 2 out; he has the physique to make more of an impact over fences. **Decor Irlandais** had a stiffish task but was below his best even so, possibly not handling the holding ground that well, not travelling quite so well as he usuallly does; held up, not fluent fifth, shaken up approaching 2 out, made no impression; his record suggests he could be the sort to be seen to advantage in a big-field handicap. **Shakem Up'arry** ought to be suited by further than 2m, but not at this level, just not good enough to hold his position when the race took shape; led, took keen hold, headed before fourth, not fluent seventh, weakened 3 out. **Getaway Fred** was out of his depth; held up, lost touch after seventh, pulled up 2 out; he's an athletic sort, likely to be effective at this trip and further at the right level and with some potential as a chaser for next season. **Son of Camas** who'd had a breathing operation since the Tolworth, was far from certain to stay this much longer trip and had to prove himself on the testing ground as well, the latter probably a factor in his failure to run much of a race, even allowing for the stiffness of his task; waited with, labouring before 3 out, pulled up next.

RSA Insurance Novices' Chase (Grade 1) (1)

Pos	*Btn*	*Horse*	*Age*	*Wgt*	*Eq*	*Trainer*	*Jockey*	*SP*
1		CHAMP (IRE)	8	11-4		Nicky Henderson	Barry Geraghty	4/1
2	1	MINELLA INDO (IRE)	7	11-4		Henry de Bromhead, Ireland	Rachael Blackmore	3/1
3	1	ALLAHO (FR)	6	11-4		W. P. Mullins, Ireland	P. Townend	5/2f
4	22	BATTLEOVERDOYEN (IRE)	7	11-4	(t)	Gordon Elliott, Ireland	Davy Russell	7/1
5	13	AYE RIGHT (IRE)	7	11-4		Harriet Graham	Callum Bewley	100/1
6	33	SLATE HOUSE (IRE)	8	11-4	(t)	Colin Tizzard	Robbie Power	20/1
F		COPPERHEAD	6	11-4		Colin Tizzard	Harry Cobden	6/1
F		EASY GAME (FR)	6	11-4		W. P. Mullins, Ireland	D. E. Mullins	10/1
ur		CASTLEBAWN WEST (IRE)	7	11-4	(h)	W. P. Mullins, Ireland	M. P. Walsh	50/1
pu		PYM (IRE)	7	11-4		Nicky Henderson	Nico de Boinville	33/1

10 ran Race Time 6m 29.20 Closing Sectional (3.75f): 59.9s (100.0%) Winning Owner: Mr John P. McManus

A remarkable finish, Champ making up 8 lengths from the last to deny a pair that had gone nip and tuck for much of the way, the trio a long way clear of the rest, no sense that the placed horses were stopping or that the winner was flattered, just that it took a while for him to be galvanised to find his full stride; there were disappointments in the race, but the first 2 were Grade 1 winners as novices over hurdles and the first 3 deserve full credit for their efforts, the form looking at least up to an average running of the RSA. **Champ** running at 3m for just the second time, maintained his unbeaten record when completing over fences, though such an eventuality looked unlikely as late as halfway up the run-in, it taking until then for him to fully find his stride, though responding in remarkable fashion once he did, making up 8 lengths from the last; waited with, mistakes twelfth and fifteenth, not quicken after 3 out, still plenty to do last, ridden and found plenty to lead final 50 yds; he's got bags of ability and, while his jumping might prove his undoing again, as it did last time, he's totally unexposed at 3m+ and has got the raw ability to make a significant impact in open company next season. **Minella Indo** was much improved on his third start over fences, showing himself well at home at this level, just as he had been over hurdles, denied a second Festival win only by a remarkable late surge by the winner; disputed lead until fifth, pressed leader after, every chance when mistake last, edged ahead final 100 yds, headed near finish; has made a really good start over fences and looks sure to win good races. **Allaho** back at 3m, has made a fine start over fences and, well backed, ran a cracker at the Festival for the second year running, giving best only late on; disputed lead, took keen hold, went on fifth, mistake twelfth, pressed on 3 out, joined when mistake last, kept on until final 50 yds; he was having just his third start over fences and may well have more to offer, a good race sure to come his way at some stage. **Battleoverdoyen** at least ran some sort of race after last season's Festival flop, but he failed to see the race out after looking a threat 3 out; held up, travelled well, headway before 3 out, chased leaders after, weakened early in straight; he's a Grade 1 winner over both hurdles and fences and a smashing looker, but perhaps is destined always to come up short in the very best races. **Aye Right** had plenty to find on form to figure in this grade, very short on experience for a race of this nature too, and he was just outclassed in the latter stages; handy, blundered sixteenth, ridden after, left behind after 3 out; he may yet do better over fences at a more realistic level. **Slate House** ran no sort of race for the second start running, his stable struggling so far to make an impact at the meeting; held up, went in snatches, mistake sixth, left behind after 3 out, hampered 2 out, finished tired. **Copperhead** had created such a good impression as he climbed the ranks this winter that it was a shame he couldn't show his form faced with his stiffest task yet, never really looking to be that comfortable and left well behind as the leaders pressed for home; prominent, pushed along fifteenth, left behind after 3 out, tailed off when fell heavily last; hopefully, he will be none the worse for this and there ought to be other days for him, particularly with long distances still to try. **Easy Game** wasn't certain to be suited by the longer trip, but he just didn't give his running, never looking likely to get involved; held up, left behind after 3 out, no chance when fell heavily last. **Castlebawn West** trying 3m for the first time over fences, needed to improve to make an impact at this level and wasn't up to the task; in rear, bad mistake fourteenth, fifth and no chance when unseated rider 2 out. **Pym** was ridden more patiently this time but fared no better, his form not good enough for this grade, though he's not run a race the last twice, which raises questions about whether he'd show his form back at the appropriate level; in touch, lost place circuit out, pulled up fourteenth.

Betway Queen Mother Champion Chase (Grade 1) (1)

Pos	*Btn*	*Horse*	*Age*	*Wgt*	*Eq*	*Trainer*	*Jockey*	*SP*
1		POLITOLOGUE (FR)	9	11-10	(t)	Paul Nicholls	Harry Skelton	6/1
2	9½	DYNAMITE DOLLARS (FR)	7	11-10		Paul Nicholls	Harry Cobden	7/1
3	3¼	BUN DORAN (IRE)	9	11-10		Tom George	Jonathan Burke	33/1
4	½	DEFI DU SEUIL (FR)	7	11-10		Philip Hobbs	Barry Geraghty	2/5f
5	32	SCEAU ROYAL (FR)	8	11-10		Alan King	Daryl Jacob	10/1

5 ran Race Time 4m 10.70 Closing Sectional (3.75f): 61.6s (96.0%) Winning Owner: Mr J. Hales

Perhaps the most eagerly-anticipated race of the Festival ended up not even featuring 2 of the main protagonists, 2-time defending champion Altior withdrawn the day before with a splint and Chacun Pour Soi ruled out on the morning of the race with an abcess; the disappointment didn't stop there either, with the one of the big 3 left standing—Defi du Seuil—turning in a lacklustre effort as odd-on favourite, leaving the path clear for Politologue—a top-class chaser but one whose limitations are well established—to dominate, hard in the circumstances to get excited about the form and indeed to avoid regretting what might've been. **Politologue** bagged his first Festival win at the fifth attempt, no match for Altior in the last 2 renewals of this but taking advantage of the absence of that rival and Chacun Pour Soi as well as the poor effort from Defi du Seuil in clinical fashion, freshened up in the 3 months since the Tingle Creek (went without his usual hood) and looking as good as ever as he dominated from the outset, jumping/travelling well in the lead, pressing on before 2 out, clear at the last, and if anything extending his advantage at the line after a brief wobble on the run-in; he'll presumably head to the Melling Chase, a race he won in 2018 before finishing second last year, though there must be a strong chance that'll take more winning, besides which he may not be the most robust nowadays (bled in the race last year as well as in this season's Tingle Creek according to his trainer). **Dynamite Dollars** gave a good account in his first open Grade 1, likely to have been a more clear-cut second but for a serious error, still time for him to advance his form a bit more granted a clearer run at things; in touch, mistake 4 out, pushed along before 2 out, secured second flat. **Bun Doran** ran as well as he was entitled, just about confirming the form he showed when winning the Desert Orchid, not the first time in recent seasons his trainer has managed to get a big-priced one placed in this race, chased leader, pushed along between last 2, lost second run-in. **Defi du Seuil** looked to have been left with an open goal after the late withdrawals of Altior and Chacun Pour Soi but fluffed his lines, never looking all that comfortable in touch on the outside and quickly in trouble once shaken up 3 out, left behind by one he'd beaten twice this season and unable even to get to a pair of inferior rivals to grab a place; obviously, this doesn't undo all the good work he'd done previously this season, but there'll be something to prove if we see him again this spring. **Sceau Royal** ran poorly, the ground perhaps an issue in a race that took more than 10 seconds longer to run than the 2019 renewal in which he was third; held up, in touch briefly 4 out, weakened after next.

Weatherbys Champion Bumper (Standard Open National Hunt Flat) (Grade 1) (1)

Pos	Btn	Horse	Age	Wgt	Eq	Trainer	Jockey	SP
1		FERNY HOLLOW (IRE)	5	11-5	(h)	W. P. Mullins, Ireland	P. Townend	11/1
2	2½	APPRECIATE IT (IRE)	6	11-5		W. P. Mullins, Ireland	Mr P. W. Mullins	15/8f
3	3¼	QUEENS BROOK (IRE)	5	10-12		Gordon Elliott, Ireland	Mr J. J. Codd	6/1
4	nk	THIRD TIME LUCKI (IRE)	5	11-5		Dan Skelton	Harry Skelton	16/1
5	hd	ESKYLANE (IRE)	6	11-5		Gordon Elliott, Ireland	Davy Russell	16/1
6	4½	OCEAN WIND	4	10-11		Roger Teal	Aidan Coleman	12/1
7	8	JULIES STOWAWAY (IRE)	6	11-5		Ms Margaret Mullins, Ireland	D. E. Mullins	40/1
8	3¾	THE GLANCING QUEEN (IRE)	6	10-12		Alan King	Tom Cannon	12/1
9	1	GOOD TIME JONNY (IRE)	5	11-5	(t)	A. J. Martin, Ireland	Robbie Power	66/1
10	½	ONE TRUE KING (IRE)	5	11-5		Nigel Twiston-Davies	Sam Twiston-Davies	100/1
11	½	FIVE BAR BRIAN (IRE)	6	11-5		W. P. Mullins, Ireland	D. J. Mullins	33/1
12	3½	MAHLER ALLSTAR (IRE)	6	11-5		Jonathan Sweeney, Ireland	M. P. Walsh	100/1
13	9	ASK A HONEY BEE (IRE)	6	11-5		Fergal O'Brien	Liam Harrison	25/1
14	1¾	CAN YOU CALL	5	11-5		Andrew Martin	Mr James Martin	100/1
15	1¼	DARLING DAUGHTER (IRE)	6	10-12		Gordon Elliott, Ireland	Ms L. O'Neill	14/1
16	nk	ADRIMEL (FR)	5	11-5	(t)	Tom Lacey	Richard Johnson	25/1
17	½	ISRAEL CHAMP (IRE)	5	11-5	(h+t)	David Pipe	Tom Scudamore	8/1
18	nk	PANIC ATTACK (IRE)	4	10-4		David Pipe	Brian Hughes	10/1
19	hd	AUDACITY	4	10-11		Warren Greatrex	Gavin Sheehan	100/1
20	hd	LET ME ENTERTAIN U	4	10-11		Michael Scudamore	Brendan Powell	100/1
21	ns	BRIEF AMBITION	6	11-5		Fergal O'Brien	Adam Wedge	100/1
22	sh	LINELEE KING (FR)	5	11-5		Olly Murphy	A. P. Heskin	100/1
23	43	SNOWPIERCER (FR)	6	11-5		Lady Susan Brooke	Miss Lorna Brooke	150/1

23 ran Race Time 4m 06.80 Closing Sectional (3.90f): 58.6s (100.2%) Winning Owner: Cheveley Park Stud

Last season's 14-runner affair proved to be just a blip, as the regular maximum-sized field lined up for the best bumper of the season, this looking a strong renewal on paper, 18 of the 23 having won last time out, the race more open than the market suggested, and it required one of the best performances in recent years, probably since Briar Hill in 2013, for the stable second string to deny the favourite as Willie Mullins landed the race for the tenth time, the big Irish stables dominating the finish, with Elliott-trained runners third and fifth, Third Time Lucki acquitting himself well in proving the pick of the British; the race was a proper test, though it is possible those that raced on the inner into the straight were at a disadvantage, Ocean Wind and, in particular, Five Bar Brian among those that should probably be marked up, the principals all among the more patiently ridden as well; as ever, this looks a race to throw up plenty of winners over hurdles next season; it was yet another race that resulted in a standing start being required. **Ferny Hollow** showed much improved form, proving well suited by the run of the race, coming right from the back of the field in a race that suited those more patiently ridden, helped too by a focused ride in the closing stages from his professional jockey; in rear, not settle fully, headway over 3f out, short of room approaching straight, stayed on to lead inside final 1f, kept on well, ridden out; he's a good prospect for novice hurdling next season, particularly at trips beyond 2m. **Appreciate It** strong in the betting, matched his improved effort last time but was run out of it by his stable companion who just seemed more clued up when it came to the crunch, still plenty to like about his prospects for jumping, probably the best of any in the race, and with the physique to go with the ability; waited with, travelled well, headway 4f out, led 3f out, shaken up straight, headed inside final 1f, kept on. **Queens Brook** confirmed debut promise, looking a smart performer, one that will do really well in mares events over hurdles next winter; held up, travelled well, headway end of back straight, pressed leader home turn, ridden soon after, not quicken final 1f. **Third Time Lucki** emerged best of the British-trained runners, putting up a smart performance; in rear, travelled well, headway 4f out, effort straight, not quicken, stayed on inside final 1f; he doesn't have quite the scope of some of the other principals, but his level of ability should ensure he wins races over hurdles next season. **Eskylane** showed much improved form, up in grade, impressing with the way he went through the race, just lacking the battle-hardened qualities required when it came to the crunch; held up, travelled well, switched gradually to the outside from the rails 4f out, headway 3f out, loomed up straight, ridden over 1f out, edged left, one paced; like all the first 5, he's a good prospect for next season. **Ocean Wind** ran creditably upped in grade, deserving a bit of extra credit for making his move on the inside, a different type to those that beat him, lacking scope and perhaps more a prospect for the Flat than hurdles; held up, effort over 3f out, not quicken home turn, kept on final 1f. **Julies Stowaway** wasn't disgraced upped in grade, just unable to sustain a good forward move as the race developed; held up, good progress 5f out, ridden 3f out, lost place soon after; he's a scopey sort and ought to make an impact over jumps next season. **The Glancing Queen** fifth in last season's renewal, shaped as if better for the run after 11 months off, having impressed with the way she moved into contention down the hill, an attempt at a repeat win in the Nickel Coin at Aintree presumably on the agenda; held up, hampered after 2f, good progress over 3f out, weakened straight. **Good Time Jonny** in first-time tongue strap, faced a stiffer task in this grade and was one of those to race around the inside from the top of the hill, likely to have been at a disadvantage as a result; held up, shaken up over 3f out, carried head bit awkwardly, plugged on straight. **One True King** was stepping up considerably in class, inexperience and luck in running playing their part in his showing; mid-division, short of room 3f out, shaken up after, ran green, outpaced;

he was one of the picks of the paddock and looks a useful novice hurdle prospect for next season. **Five Bar Brian** couldn't repeat the form he showed on his return, faced with a much stiffer task, but he shaped a fair bit better than the bare result, down the inside towards the straight, but going as well as any before position and greenness told; mid-division, tanked along, headway over 4f out, close up approaching home turn, ridden after, no extra over 1f out; interesting prospect. **Mahler Allstar** had a lot on in this grade; prominent, led over 4f out, headed 3f out, weakened straight. **Ask A Honey Bee** had won his first 3 starts in bumpers, but ran poorly in the best race he'd contested, perhaps doing a bit more than ideal; prominent, ridden over 4f out, left behind before straight. **Can You Call** was well held after 3 months off, just out of his depth; chased leaders until halfway. **Darling Daughter** lost her unbeaten record, unimpressive in appearance and perhaps just finding the tougher company beyond her; prominent, ridden over 4f out, lost place before home turn. **Adrimel** was well held, doing a bit too much up with the pace; handy, took keen hold, every chance over 3f out, weakened early in straight; he'd created a good impression previously and very much looks the part for jumping, one of the 3 or 4 best-looking runners in a good field. **Israel Champ** had created such a good impression in winning his last 2 starts, but disappointed, leading in this company a different task altogether; led, pushed along end of back straight, headed over 4f out, weakened soon after; he still has potential for novice hurdles next season. **Panic Attack** on first outing since leaving Willie Mullins after 8 weeks off, went backwards from debut, softer ground and a greater emphasis on stamina likely factors, though she's nothing much on looks and may well struggle to repeat that initial win in mares company; waited with, pushed along over 3f out, left behind soon after. **Audacity** was well held, running poorly for the second start running, his Cheltenham form, when he was enterprisingly ridden, remaining a standout; pushed along from standing start to take a prominent position, labouring end of back straight, tailed off 3f out. **Let Me Entertain U** found the step up to this level so soon way too much; mid-division, off the bridle long way out, tailed off 3f out. **Brief Ambition** was well held, faced with his stiffest task to date; waited with, pushed along 3f out, weakened soon after. **Linelee King** was well held, lacking the experience to make any impact; held up, not settle fully, pushed along over 5f out, left behind 3f out; he's an athletic sort and clearly well regarded, connections having subsequently bought the horse that beat him when he was odds on at Chepstow. **Snowpiercer** was way out of his depth; raced off the pace, left behind over 5f out.

CHELTENHAM Thursday March 12

SOFT

Marsh Novices' Chase (Golden Miller) (Grade 1) (1)

Pos	Btn	Horse	Age	Wgt	Eq	Trainer	Jockey	SP
1		SAMCRO (IRE)	8	11-4	(t)	Gordon Elliott, Ireland	Davy Russell	4/1
2	ns	MELON	8	11-4	(s)	W. P. Mullins, Ireland	Mr P. W. Mullins	14/1
3	1	FAUGHEEN (IRE)	12	11-4		W. P. Mullins, Ireland	P. Townend	3/1f
4	3¼	MISTER FISHER (IRE)	6	11-4		Nicky Henderson	Nico de Boinville	7/1
5	4¾	TORNADO FLYER (IRE)	7	11-4		W. P. Mullins, Ireland	D. E. Mullins	10/1
6	1¼	MIDNIGHT SHADOW	7	11-4		Sue Smith	Danny Cook	22/1
7	2¾	SAINT SONNET (FR)	5	11-3		Paul Nicholls	Harry Cobden	33/1
8	12	BAPAUME (FR)	7	11-4	(t)	W. P. Mullins, Ireland	Rachael Blackmore	20/1
9	40	ANNIE MC (IRE)	6	10-11		Jonjo O'Neill	Jonjo O'Neill Jr.	18/1

10	16	POKER PLAY (FR)	7	11-4	(b)	David Pipe	Tom Scudamore	100/1
ur		ITCHY FEET (FR)	6	11-4		Olly Murphy	Gavin Sheehan	7/2
pu		RESERVE TANK (IRE)	6	11-4		Colin Tizzard	Robbie Power	12/1

12 ran Race Time 5m 07.50 Closing Sectional (4.00f): 57.8s (107.7%) Winning Owner: Gigginstown House Stud

The first 3 might have taken their time in going over fences, the first 2 both older than any previous winner since the race's inception in 2011 and the third long since into the veteran stage, but that clearly hasn't prevented them making the grade as chasers—indeed Faugheen came into this with the joint-highest Timeform rating of any previous runner in the race's history; this was the second novice chase of the week dominated by Irish-trained runners, a prominent pitch an advantage as is so often the case in this. **Samcro** looked to have the world at his feet when landing the Baring Bingham at this meeting 2 years earlier but things hadn't gone to plan since, and while this second Festival success isn't conclusive proof that he'll go to the very top over fences, it was yet another advertisement for the training skills of Gordon Elliott, Samcro apparently not easy to train but primed to perfection 11 weeks on from a tame-finishing second to Faugheen at Christmas (since when he'd had another breathing operation); never far away, he edged ahead still on the bridle early in the straight, lost the lead when hitting 2 out only to regain it at the last, all out to hold on from a rallying Melon, the line coming at just the right time. **Melon** second in a Supreme and 2 Champion Hurdles, suffered his most agonising Festival defeat yet as he was forced to fill the same spot for a fourth year running, going with zest back in headgear and leading before the fifth but ultimately undone by a failure to see a stride at the last (headed briefly early in the straight before jumping on again 2 out), and even then he fought back to nose ahead once more a stride from the line only for the photo to favour Samcro; one solitary odds-on Grade 2 hurdle to go with a pair of maiden wins (hurdle and chase) isn't the reward his talents justify, and perhaps he could start to rectify that at Punchestown. **Faugheen** has never been a normal horse, winner of a 3m graded novice hurdle in the mud before winning the Champion Hurdle the season after, and although his reinvention as a chaser wasn't quite complete with a third Festival victory, to sustain the level of form he has at the age of 12 is some achievement; having led early, he chased the leader from the fifth but wasn't always fluent, his most costly blemish coming when in close and pecking 3 out meaning he was caught behind the leaders turning for home and unable to quite get back to them, switched outside on the run-in having initially explored a gap up the inside before the last. **Mister Fisher** improved his rating in emerging best of the British 7 weeks on from Doncaster, and might have reduced the deficit to the Irish trio ahead with a clearer run down the hill; settled in touch, he travelled fluently but untidy jumps at the fifth and the ninth were a precursor to him drifting back before 3 out, having to pick his way through as he made headway early in the straight and running on to the line, confirming himself fully effective at 2½m. **Tornado Flyer** ran to a similar level to last time in another Grade 1, the race not fully getting to the bottom of him, either; patiently ridden, he was untidy at the seventh and not fluent 3 out when still having plenty to do, nearest at the finish having been only eighth 2 out. **Midnight Shadow** is holding his form well and gave a good account of himself for a long way; raced wide in mid-division, went handy 3 out and briefly looked a threat but couldn't quicken between the last 2. **Saint Sonnet** faced a huge rise in class after winning a small-field novice at prohibitive odds at Catterick and acquitted himself well for a long way, his position on the heels of the leading bunch going well turning for home a better snapshot of his potential for next season than his finishing position, particularly as he'd made quite a bad mistake at the eleventh; there's better to come as he matures, and he'd be a very interesting contender were he pointed the way of the Bet Victor back here in the autumn. **Bapaume** failed to find the step back up in trip or the return to Cheltenham (third in the 2017 Triumph and fourth in the 2019 Stayers' Hurdle) sparking him back to life to any significant degree; mid-field, untidy tenth, shaken up 3 out, not quicken entering straight, left behind from 2 out. **Annie Mc** had done her winning in very small fields and found this a baptism of fire; held up on outer, effort when bad mistake 4 out, brief headway approaching home turn, effort flattened out. **Poker Play** was out of his depth with first-time blinkers replacing his usual cheekpieces after 10 weeks off/a breathing operation; chased leaders until eighth, behind eleventh. **Itchy Feet** had coped well with the demands of Sandown's fences in winning the Scilly Isles but found his jumping not standing the test this time, unseating his rider at the sixth when off the pace having already made a mistake at the fourth; he remains open to improvement. **Reserve Tank** was backed at long odds returning from 3 months off but proved to be a disappointment; tracked pace, not fluent seventh, lost ground eleventh, untidy 3 out, left behind quickly.

Ryanair Chase (Festival Trophy) (Grade 1) (1)

Pos	Btn	Horse	Age	Wgt	Eq	Trainer	Jockey	SP
1		MIN (FR)	9	11-10		W. P. Mullins, Ireland	P. Townend	2/1
2	nk	SAINT CALVADOS (FR)	7	11-10		Harry Whittington	Gavin Sheehan	16/1
3	1½	A PLUS TARD (FR)	6	11-10		Henry de Bromhead, Ireland	Rachael Blackmore	7/4f
4	13	FRODON (FR)	8	11-10	(t)	Paul Nicholls	Bryony Frost	11/2
5	nk	DUC DES GENIEVRES (FR)	7	11-10	(t)	W. P. Mullins, Ireland	Robbie Power	18/1
6	8½	SHATTERED LOVE (IRE)	9	11-3	(s+t)	Gordon Elliott, Ireland	M. P. Walsh	20/1
7	35	ASO (FR)	10	11-10	(b)	Venetia Williams	Charlie Deutsch	25/1
F		RIDERS ONTHE STORM (IRE)	7	11-10		Nigel Twiston-Davies	Sam Twiston-Davies	11/1

8 ran Race Time 5m 20.00 Closing Sectional (4.0f): 61.2s (101.6%) Winning Owner: Mrs S. Ricci

An up-to-scratch Ryanair, Min well established as top-class and chased home by an improver and the well-backed favourite, the trio separating themselves from the rest in a well-run race. **Min** is a reliable top-class performer and bagged the Festival win his record deserved, no progress required on form that already set the standard but showcasing all his best qualities, jumping/travelling well under a positive ride (led from eighth), outjumping A Plus Tard 2 out after that rival had briefly threatened to challenge then driven out as the runner-up tried to close after the last; he was devastating in the Melling Chase last year and another bold bid there seems all but assured. **Saint Calvados** has improved for more patient tactics/step up in trip and proved himself a borderline top-class chaser stepping back out of handicap company, creeping into it around the inner after 3 out, moving into second before the last, where a mistake checked his momentum briefly, then closing the gap to the winner from 2 lengths despite being forced to switch from off the rail, enough going wrong for him in the closing stages that connections will no doubt relish another crack at the winner at Aintree. **A Plus Tard** was strong in the betting back up in trip at a track where he was so impressive in handicap company last season and ran his race without seeming to have any excuses, coming there to challenge before 2 out but one paced from the last; he's still a relative youngster and is sure to win plenty more good races. **Frodon** never looked like repeating his 2019 win in this race, unable to get into the same rhythm up against these faster horses, losing the lead as early as the fifth and soon beaten once the leaders pressed on 3 out. **Duc des Genievres** wasn't disgraced but hasn't gone on from last season's Arkle win, his jumping average at best, a Grade 1 win in open company beyond him on the evidence of this season; held up, hit fifth, mistake 4 out, ridden before 2 out, no further impression. **Shattered Love** found this too competitive; chased leaders, ridden after 3 out, weakened. **Aso** ran poorly in first-time blinkers after 11 weeks off, seemingly not the same force this season as when placed in this in 2019 and 2017; raced wide, close up, not fluent eighth, lost place before 5 out, struggling after next. **Riders Onthe Storm** was still going okay held up when falling 3 out, though it wasn't his first mistake that did for him (also hit tenth and 5 out).

Paddy Power Stayers' Hurdle (Grade 1) (1)

Pos	*Btn*	*Horse*	*Age*	*Wgt*	*Eq*	*Trainer*	*Jockey*	*SP*
1		LISNAGAR OSCAR (IRE)	7	11-10		Rebecca Curtis	Adam Wedge	50/1
2	2	RONALD PUMP	7	11-10	(h+t)	Matthew J. Smith, Ireland	B. J. Cooper	20/1
3	3	BACARDYS (FR)	9	11-10		W. P. Mullins, Ireland	Mr P. W. Mullins	33/1
4	¾	EMITOM (IRE)	6	11-10		Warren Greatrex	Gavin Sheehan	10/1
5	½	SUMMERVILLE BOY (IRE)	8	11-10		Tom George	Jonathan Burke	10/1
6	1¾	TOBEFAIR	10	11-10		Debra Hamer	Tom Bellamy	50/1
7	6½	PAISLEY PARK (IRE)	8	11-10		Emma Lavelle	Aidan Coleman	4/6f
8	3	APPLE'S JADE (FR)	8	11-3	(b+t)	Gordon Elliott, Ireland	Richard Johnson	7/1
9	18	THE JAM MAN (IRE)	7	11-10		Ronan M. P. McNally, Ireland	Sean Flanagan	50/1
10	½	ASK DILLON (IRE)	7	11-10	(s)	Fergal O'Brien	Jonjo O'Neill Jr.	66/1
pu		CITY ISLAND (IRE)	7	11-10	(t)	Martin Brassil, Ireland	M. P. Walsh	14/1
pu		DONNA'S DIAMOND (IRE)	11	11-10		Chris Grant	Thomas Dowson	100/1
pu		L'AMI SERGE (IRE)	10	11-10		Nicky Henderson	Daryl Jacob	50/1
pu		PENHILL	9	11-10		W. P. Mullins, Ireland	P. Townend	10/1
pu		WEST APPROACH	10	11-10	(s)	Colin Tizzard	Harry Cobden	100/1

15 ran Race Time 6m 02.20 Closing Sectional (3.7f): 60s (93.2%) Winning Owner: Racing for Fun

What promised to be the crowning of another multiple winner of the Stayers' Hurdle was blown wide open by Paisley Park's unexpected misstep, with a bunch of upstart handicappers and static and exposed graded performers making up the bulk of those who featured in an unusually bunched finish, the first sextet covered by only 8 lengths at the line; despite the outgoing Apple's Jade being ignored in a clear lead, the main pack still reached the sixth around 2 seconds faster than the leader in the far more slowly-run Pertemps, though things still got messy as the field closed up again before the race unfolded from 2 out, Paisley Park suffering most as some of the lesser lights shut the door. **Lisnagar Oscar** delivered at the Festival a year after something similar had been expected in some quarters in the Albert Bartlett, the key beneficiary of Paisley Park's no-show for all this goes down as a big step forward on his part as well, not putting a foot wrong in seeing off the rather second-rate stayers who remained as threats, making smooth headway out wide to lead early in the straight and keeping on well; it's doubtful this will signal a spell of dominance in the division, heavy odds against he'd beat Paisley Park were they to meet again, even unlikely to be favourite on form to beat Sire du Berlais judged on the latter's Pertemps performance earlier in the day. **Ronald Pump** produced another personal best in a career full of them, clearly more at home in this sphere than chasing, the gap from handicaps to the best staying hurdlers around not proving so vast as it might normally be given the current substandard scene, made worse of course by the clubhouse leader's disappointing display; patiently ridden, he jumped sketchily as per but made smooth headway 2 out and stalked the leader running to the last, hindered by another error there but beaten on merit all the same given how he was held by the winner after. **Bacardys** made a much better fist of things than in this a year earlier following a refreshing 11-week break, even deserving extra credit under a ride that saw him left with a lot to do, the effort of closing seemingly telling on him; patiently ridden, avoided mistakes, travelled well, off pace still 2 out and only tenth entering straight, rapid headway out wide before last, no further impression; his proximity, aged 9, in a Stayers' Hurdle does give further reason to rate the form on the low side, however. **Emitom** couldn't raise his game still further but still has time on his side, a relative youth—and lightly raced—compared to most on the staying scene, a few creases yet to be ironed out as well; mid-division, blundered 2 out, ridden after, effort on inner straight, stayed on gradually. **Summerville Boy** possibly failed to stay in a more strongly-run race at this trip 7 weeks on from the Cleeve, reversing form with the disappointing favourite but failing to uphold it with Lisnagar Oscar; prominent main group but not settle fully, going well when blundered 2 out, pushed along straight, one paced. **Tobefair** typically gave his running after 7 weeks off, his best just not enough in this company; mid-division, outpaced between 3 out and 2 out, rallied gradually straight. **Paisley Park** will have a chance to join the likes of Baracouda, Inglis Drever and Big Buck's if back in one piece as a 9-y-o next season but this was very much one that got away in a weak staying hurdle scene over which he's ruled for well over a year, clearly not firing for whatever reason and hindered as well by a troubled passage as he sought to make his trademark surge after 2 out, clear by the time they reached the last that it wasn't there for once, even weakening by the finish while a rival he'd beaten convincingly in the Cleeve was causing a shock up ahead; he remains the best in the division, despite this first blemish, though connections might have to explore headgear in order to bridge the negative impact of his customary lazy streak. **Apple's Jade** was lit up in first-time blinkers after 7 weeks off and, ridden aggressively, ran herself into the ground, connections quick to draw stumps on her career in the aftermath; raced clear, took strong hold, reduced advantage after 3 out, headed early in straight, dropped away; she'd lost a good bit in terms of ability and consistency this season, but that shouldn't detract from a stellar record featuring 15 wins, all bar 4 of which came at Grade 1 level; she's reportedly to visit Walk In The Park. **The Jam Man** wasn't up to the task above all, never involved stepping out of handicaps. **Ask Dillon** failed to improve for a change of tactics or fitting of cheekpieces, though there'll be more suitable testing grounds than this for such experiments; prominent main group, chased leader from sixth, ridden after 3 out, lost place when blundered next. **City Island** has hit the skids since edging out Champ in the Ballymore at this meeting in 2019, chasing failing on the whole and this return to hurdles prompting a far-from-robust display, lack of stamina/fitness upped in trip after 2 months off less likely excuses than a potential physical issue (had breathing operation prior to this); patiently ridden, smooth headway 2 out, yet to be asked for effort when approaching home turn, shaken up straight but went to nothing and even pulled up before the last. **Donna's Diamond** who needed to find plenty of improvement, went backwards from a gruelling reappearance in any case; led main group, lost place when blundered sixth, struggling 3 out. **L'Ami Serge** is ever so easy to oppose these days; held up, shaken up before 2 out, no response.

Penhill was pulled up lame soon after a blunder at the third. **West Approach** in first-time cheekpieces, ran one of this season's poorer races regardless of the stiffness of his task; held up, lost ground from 3 out, no response.

CHELTENHAM Friday March 13
GOOD to SOFT

JCB Triumph Hurdle (Grade 1) (1)

Pos	Btn	Horse	Age	Wgt	Eq	Trainer	Jockey	SP
1		BURNING VICTORY (FR)	4	10-7		W. P. Mullins, Ireland	P. Townend	12/1
2	2¾	ASPIRE TOWER (IRE)	4	11-0		Henry de Bromhead, Ireland	Rachael Blackmore	5/1
3	¾	ALLMANKIND	4	11-0	(h+t)	Dan Skelton	Harry Skelton	7/2
4	¾	NAVAJO PASS	4	11-0		Donald McCain	Brian Hughes	50/1
5	½	SIR PSYCHO (IRE)	4	11-0	(s)	Paul Nicholls	Bryony Frost	16/1
6	1¼	CERBERUS	4	11-0	(t)	Joseph Patrick O'Brien, Ireland	M. P. Walsh	20/1
7	nk	A WAVE OF THE SEA (IRE)	4	11-0		Joseph Patrick O'Brien, Ireland	Barry Geraghty	12/1
8	4	SOLO (FR)	4	11-0		Paul Nicholls	Harry Cobden	4/1
9	1½	NEVER DO NOTHING (IRE)	4	11-0		John McConnell, Ireland	D. J. McInerney	100/1
10	6	LORD LAMINGTON	4	11-0		Alan King	Tom Cannon	100/1
11	11	HOOK UP (FR)	4	10-7	(t)	W. P. Mullins, Ireland	D. E. Mullins	33/1
12	44	YELLOW TIGER (FR)	4	11-0	(t)	David Loughnane	Alain Cawley	100/1
ur		GOSHEN (FR)	4	11-0		Gary Moore	Jamie Moore	5/2f

13 ran Race Time 4m 07.40 Closing Sectional (3.70f): 58.5s (93.1%) Winning Owner: Mrs Audrey Turley

This looked a strong renewal of the Triumph beforehand, with as many as 4 having looked well up to the standard required for an average running, one of that quartet, Goshen, set to win in impressive fashion when he lost his rider at the last, potentially the best winner of the race since the ill-fated Our Conor; the pace had been relentless and most were in trouble a long way out, that Goshen had been up with the pace all to his credit, the lucky winner coming from the back of the field and improving significantly on her debut form, the first filly to win the Triumph since Snow Drop in 2000, the placed pair, who'd been involved in forcing the pace, better than the result indicates. **Burning Victory** built on debut promise, showing herself a useful young hurdler, even though a fortunate winner on the day, well suited by the way the race was run too; in rear, took keen hold, mistake fourth, good progress after 2 out, well held in second when left in front last, kept on well, ridden out; she's clearly got the potential to progress again, an athletic sort and more of a stayer than might be suspected from her pedigree, perhaps the Mares Hurdle her likely aim another year. **Aspire Tower** ran creditably, just paying for being too involved in forcing the pace and unable to finish so well as the winner once the race was opened up by Goshen's departure; jumped left, pulled hard, disputed lead early, remained prominent, outpaced before 2 out, left third and jumped left last, stayed on to take second close home. **Allmankind** shaped really well after 11 weeks off, away from really testing ground, surely doing too much up front; forced pace, pushed along from third, headed 2 out, weakened approaching last, left every chance there, hung right, no extra near finish; he remains with plenty of potential. **Navajo Pass** after 3 months off, seemed to excel himself, despite sweating and being on his toes beforehand; tracked pace, outpaced before 2 out, kept on straight; he's done well so far over hurdles and has the potential to do even better when he goes up in trip. **Sir Psycho** seemed to excel himself, up in grade, well served by the way the race was run; close up when hampered first, settled in touch, effort approaching 2 out, not quicken straight; he's a useful hurdler, with the physique to go on and in a stable that will get the maximum out of him. **Cerberus** wasn't disgraced, particularly given his jumping left plenty to be desired; held up, mistakes fifth and 3 out, labouring 2 out, held when mistake last; he lacks scope, which may limit his long-term potential. **A Wave of The Sea** ought to have been suited by the run of the race, given the way he won at Leopardstown, but he couldn't land a blow, running a bit below that form; held up, some headway 3 out, not quicken after next; he was one of the most experienced in the field and looks just a useful hurdler, though his physique promises a future outside juvenile company. **Solo** was understandably ridden with more restraint than in the Adonis, but proved a disappointment, perhaps not suited by the track; in touch, travelled well, not fluent 2 out, ridden straight, found little; perhaps his form at Kempton isn't so good as it looked at the time, but he is worth another chance to disprove that. **Never Do Nothing** showed much more like his debut form, though he wasn't up to the grade; waited with, labouring before 2 out. **Lord Lamington** was simply out of his depth; raced off the pace, labouring before 2 out. **Hook Up** went backwards from her highly promising debut, behind the winner at Fairyhouse; held up, labouring 2 out. **Yellow Tiger** found this way too competitive at an early stage of his career; held up, labouring after 3 out. **Goshen** strong in the betting and with his form boosted from last time, would have won convincingly had he jumped the last, a real shame that he couldn't show what he could do after he'd been up with the strong pace and was still finding plenty when he went, any concerns about his jumping ironically quickly dismissed, as until the last he had jumped straight and true; tracked pace, took keen hold, switched outside early final circuit, led 2 out, forged clear, in command, 10 lengths up, when blundered and unseated rider last; he would have been an above-average winner of the Triumph and looks set to make an impact in open company next season, every chance that he will prove even better when he goes up in trip.

Albert Bartlett Novices' Hurdle (Spa) (Grade 1) (1)

Pos	Btn	Horse	Age	Wgt	Eq	Trainer	Jockey	SP
1		MONKFISH (IRE)	6	11-5		W. P. Mullins, Ireland	P. Townend	5/1
2	nk	LATEST EXHIBITION (IRE)	7	11-5		Paul Nolan, Ireland	B. J. Cooper	9/2
3	ns	FURY ROAD (IRE)	6	11-5	(t)	Gordon Elliott, Ireland	Davy Russell	5/1
4	1¼	THYME HILL	6	11-5		Philip Hobbs	Richard Johnson	4/1f
5	10	JANIDIL (FR)	6	11-5		W. P. Mullins, Ireland	M. P. Walsh	16/1
6	2½	SEMPO (IRE)	6	11-5	(t)	Joseph Patrick O'Brien, Ireland	J. J. Slevin	12/1
7	4½	THE WOLF (FR)	6	11-5		Olly Murphy	Aidan Coleman	100/1
8	½	HOUSE ISLAND (IRE)	6	11-5		Paul Webber	Gavin Sheehan	66/1
9	¾	FOXY JACKS (IRE)	6	11-5	(s)	M. F. Morris, Ireland	Philip Enright	100/1
10	2½	AIONE (FR)	7	11-5		W. P. Mullins, Ireland	D. E. Mullins	33/1
11	13	THE CASHEL MAN (IRE)	8	11-5	(b)	Nicky Henderson	Jeremiah McGrath	25/1
12	1	OSCAR ACADEMY (IRE)	7	11-5		Gavin Patrick Cromwell, Ireland	Jonathan Moore	100/1
13	15	RAMSES DE TEILLEE (FR)	8	11-5	(t)	David Pipe	Tom Scudamore	12/1
14	3¼	REDFORD ROAD	6	11-5		Nigel Twiston-Davies	Sam Twiston-Davies	40/1
pu		CAT TIGER (FR)	6	11-5	(t)	Paul Nicholls	Mr David Maxwell	50/1
pu		COBBLER'S WAY (IRE)	6	11-5	(t)	Henry de Bromhead, Ireland	Rachael Blackmore	14/1
pu		HARRY SENIOR (IRE)	6	11-5		Colin Tizzard	Robbie Power	16/1
pu		KILTEALY BRIGGS (IRE)	6	11-5	(t)	Jamie Snowden	A. P. Heskin	100/1
pu		LIEUTENANT ROCCO (IRE)	5	11-5		Colin Tizzard	Harry Cobden	33/1

19 ran Race Time 5m 59.00 Closing Sectional (3.70f): 53.6s (103.4%) Winning Owner: Mrs S. Ricci

A more sensible pace than anticipated made this not quite the slog it can sometimes be, the first 4 all seeing the race out strongly and producing an exciting finish, any of the quartet a plausible winner were the race re-run under the same circumstances, hard to take a really high view of the form, though all 4 should make an impact next season, as so often this a smashing field on looks with any number potential chasing prospects at a good level. **Monkfish** was taking a big step up in class, but took that in his stride, impressing with the way he went through the race and his willingness in the finish, a chaser on looks and a smashing prospect for next winter, the RSA an obvious aim; travelled well, disputed lead early, remained prominent, blundered eighth, led again soon after 2 out, edged right before last, headed run-in, rallied to lead again close home. **Latest Exhibition** doesn't have the physique of the first and third, but he has as much ability as a hurdler, confirming himself a smart novice, giving best only late on over this longer trip; mid-division, travelled well, good progress 3 out, challenged last, edged ahead run-in, headed final 50 yds, stayed on. **Fury Road** ran a fine race, his best yet, well suited by the extra demands on stamina, clearly a smart novice and a prospective even better chaser for next season, just about the pick of the field on looks; in touch, headway approaching 2 out, ridden home turn, edged right, challenged last, stayed on to lead final 50 yds, headed close home. **Thyme Hill** upped in trip, was well backed, despite his stable having 2 leading contenders flop earlier in the week, and he acquitted himself really well, likely to have done even better with the rub of the green, the gap closing on him as he was moving forward approaching the last, losing momentum as a result; held up, travelled well, smooth headway 2 out, short of room approaching last, switched, ridden, hampered again run-in, not quicken final 100 yds; he's done well over hurdles and, like plenty of the other principals, will make a smashing chaser next season, judged on looks. **Janidil** after 3 months off, up in grade, shaped better than the bare result, making his move after the principals and his stamina running on empty late on over this much longer trip; held up, travelled well, headway 2 out, chased leaders approaching last, one paced; he's an interesting prospect for chasing next season. **Sempo** sixth in last year's Champion Bumper, hasn't really filled out over the last year, but he ran respectably in much the toughest race he's contested, essentially not good enough (should be suited by the trip); mid-division, took keen hold, effort after 2 out, kept on. **The Wolf** was an optimistic runner at this level and wasn't up to the task, running about as well as could be expected; mid-field, took keen hold, headway before 2 out, not fluent there, soon done with. **House Island** probably wasn't good enough anyway, but lack of stamina meant that he ran below his best; helped set pace, led third, headed sixth, led again eighth, headed 2 out, weakened straight. **Foxy Jacks** seemed likely to be suited by the return to further, but he had plenty on up in grade and just wasn't up to the task; held up, took keen hold, effort 2 out, made little impression. **Aione** was beaten by more than the markedly longer trip; held up, effort 2 out, made little impression; he has plenty about him physically and ought to make a useful chaser next season. **The Cashel Man** a different type to nearly all the others, having come from the Flat, could be given a chance on his form against Thyme Hill, but he ran no sort of race, in trouble a long way out. **Oscar Academy** was well held on first outing since leaving Olly Murphy for £70,000, far too keen to give himself any chance of seeing the race out; in touch, chased leaders fifth, pulled way to front next, joined after seventh, weakened straight. **Ramses de Teillee** was well held, easy enough to excuse this effort, a much more patient ride away from the mud unlikely to show him to advantage; in touch, close up when mistake 3 out, every chance next, weakened. **Redford Road** seemed likely to be suited by the return to 3m, but ran poorly, under pressure before most; held up, ridden 3 out, made no impression. **Cat Tiger** upped in trip and grade, cut no ice, tried in a tongue strap for the first time in Britain, at least; held up, mistake third, left behind 2 out, pulled up before last. **Cobbler's Way** would have run below form had he not appeared to go wrong on the run to the last, hopefully none the worse long term, as he very much has the look of a better chaser; prominent, ridden before 2 out, no extra early in straight, pulled up before last, lame. **Harry Senior** seemed likely to be effective over the longer trip and might well be another day, his chance gone with a blunder before halfway, easy to put a line through this run; mid-division, bad mistake fifth, lost touch halfway, pulled up before eighth. **Kiltealy Briggs** was geed up beforehand and didn't run much of a race, facing his stiffest task to date; held up, left behind 2 out, pulled up straight. **Lieutenant Rocco** really looks the part and has stamina in his pedigree, but this was a big step up in trip and as big a climb in grade and he just wasn't up to the task; took keen hold, led first, remained prominent, weakened 2 out, pulled up straight.

Magners Cheltenham Gold Cup Chase (Grade 1) (1)

Pos	*Btn*	*Horse*	*Age*	*Wgt*	*Eq*	*Trainer*	*Jockey*	*SP*
1		AL BOUM PHOTO (FR)	8	11-10		W. P. Mullins, Ireland	P. Townend	10/3f
2	nk	SANTINI	8	11-10	(s)	Nicky Henderson	Nico de Boinville	5/1
3	1¼	LOSTINTRANSLATION (IRE)	8	11-10	(t)	Colin Tizzard	Robbie Power	10/1
4	nk	MONALEE (IRE)	9	11-10		Henry de Bromhead, Ireland	Rachael Blackmore	20/1
5	4½	DELTA WORK (FR)	7	11-10	(h+t)	Gordon Elliott, Ireland	M. P. Walsh	5/1
6	1	REAL STEEL (FR)	7	11-10		W. P. Mullins, Ireland	Brian Hughes	50/1
7	4¾	KEMBOY (FR)	8	11-10		W. P. Mullins, Ireland	Mr P. W. Mullins	8/1
8	5	CLAN DES OBEAUX (FR)	8	11-10		Paul Nicholls	Harry Cobden	7/1
9	1¼	BRISTOL DE MAI (FR)	9	11-10		Nigel Twiston-Davies	Daryl Jacob	18/1
10	sh	CHRIS'S DREAM (IRE)	8	11-10		Henry de Bromhead, Ireland	Aidan Coleman	20/1
11	nk	ELEGANT ESCAPE (IRE)	8	11-10		Colin Tizzard	Jonjo O'Neill Jr.	66/1
F		PRESENTING PERCY	9	11-10	(t)	Patrick G. Kelly, Ireland	Davy Russell	10/1

12 ran Race Time 6m 51.30 Closing Sectional (4.00f): 57.8s (108.1%) Winning Owner: Mrs J. Donnelly

A representative field for the most prestigious race in jumping, only Native River of the main trial winners missing, the runners all aged between 7 and 9 and thus in theory in their prime, the race an enthralling one to watch, with all bar Elegant Escape in with a chance 3 out after the pace had been just fair, fine margins between the principals and a case for saying quite a few might win another day on different ground, or with a race run differently, or another track or just with more rub of the green, but the winner, albeit narrowly, was the right one on the day, the first back-to-back Gold Cup winner since Best Mate won his third in 2004, not by any means the best winner in that period but one primed for the day on both occasions and given a copybook ride that enabled him to run to his best, the proximity of the fourth and sixth making it difficult to rate the form as better than an average Gold Cup; Al Boum Photo gave his trainer a 4-timer on the card, including all 3 Grade 1 races, making it 5 championship races on the week, the best races dominated by the top yards, with Henderson, de Bromhead, Elliott and Nicholls winning 7 between them, leaving just the Stayers' Hurdle for one of the smaller yards, Elliott dominant through strength of numbers in the 'lesser races', including winning 4 handicaps, which at least means we should hear less about undeniable facts next year, the difficulty of less powerful yards getting a look in and the underperformance of some of the top British yards, aside from Henderson, perhaps more fruitful topics of discussion, though the shadow looming over the whole event was the wisdom in its taking place, at least in front of such large crowds, the answer to that question not yet knowable. **Al Boum Photo** followed the same route to Gold Cup success as he had the previous season, trained to the minute and given the ideal ride in a race which played to his strengths, his jumping largely an asset and the way he travelled meaning he could get into the best position when the tempo lifted from 3 out, this probably the best guide to his merit, showing him a top-class chaser, a game and genuine one, but not an outstanding one; patiently ridden, travelled well, mistake thirteenth, headway 5 out, led next, headed briefly home turn, joined 2 out, kept on well run-in, had nothing to spare; he's young enough to think a third win in this race is a distinct possibility. **Santini** in first-time cheekpieces, ran as well as he ever has, just lacking the pace of the winner at a crucial stage, but emerging with his reputation enhanced; handy, led briefly before 4 out, again approaching straight, not quicken between last 2, switched soon after last, edged left, kept on well final 100 yds, just failed. **Lostintranslation** who'd had a breathing operation since his King George flop and was in a first-time tongue strap, ran a cracker, much the brightest spot in the week for his yard, looking the winner briefly on the turn but not so strong in the final 1f as the winner; in touch, jumped well, took keen hold, headway on bridle 4 out, disputed lead next, not quicken final 100 yds; the Bowl at Aintree would be the obvious next race. **Monalee** ran much better than he did in the Ryanair the previous March, coping well with the demands of the race and showing plenty of stamina, just lacking a turn of foot at a crucial stage, likely to have been third in a few more strides; prominent, travelled well, led fourteenth, headed when impeded before 4 out, not quicken straight, carried right run-in, stayed on. **Delta Work** ran creditably, though his jumping let him down, to an even greater extent than it had when he was third in the RSA last season, just making too many mistakes to get into an ideal rhythm; held up, jumped none too fluently, ridden sixteenth, headway when mistake eighteenth, stayed on straight, mistake last, no extra late on; he was one of the joint-youngest in the field and will continue to make an impact at the highest level, with every chance he'll go close with a better round at Punchestown. **Real Steel** upped markedly in trip, ran a remarkable race, belying his unconsidered status, performing as well as he ever has, though clearly running out of stamina late on; dropped out, travelled strongly, headway on bridle 3 out, shaken up 2 out, no extra; he did well enough to think he'd be a serious contender in the Ryanair another year. **Kemboy** had unseated early in last year's Gold Cup and, though he got around this time, his jumping let him down again, just making too many errors to get competitive; jumped none too fluently, led first, remained prominent, lost place eighth, labouring after 3 out, plugged on run-in; he's as good as any of these on his day and may well bounce back at Aintree and/or Punchestown, assuming they go ahead. **Clan des Obeaux** wasn't in the same form as last time, unlike in last season's Gold Cup not failing possibly through want of stamina, just not running his race; waited with, not fluent seventeenth, pushed along after, left behind before straight. **Bristol de Mai** a good third in the 2019 renewal, was below form this time, not obviously let down by his jumping; jumped on second, made most until fourteenth, mistake seventeenth, ridden after, weakened straight. **Chris's Dream** seemed not to get home, the way he went through the race promising more than he delivered; patiently ridden, travelled well, ridden approaching 2 out, found little. **Elegant Escape** had a stiff task up in grade; prominent, led briefly after second, not fluent third, pushed along fourteenth, lost place eighteenth, lost touch 3 out. **Presenting Percy** was likely to have run creditably had he completed, perhaps finishing somewhere around fifth or sixth, depending on how well he stayed on; held up, travelled well, mistake eighteenth, headway early in straight, ridden when fell 2 out.

TIMEFORM'S BEST OF 2019/20

Altior and Tiger Roll took centre stage in our review of the 2018/19 National Hunt season, but that pair had to settle for minor roles this time, with both being forced to miss major targets for one reason or another. Tiger Roll's tilt at winning a third successive Grand National was ended when the Aintree meeting was called off due to the Covid-19 pandemic, while the Cheltenham Festival went ahead but without Altior, who was ruled out of his own hat-trick bid in the Queen Mother Champion Chase at the eleventh hour due to a minor setback. Altior is already a three-time winner of Timeform's Horse of the Year award, but he forfeited that title in the latest season to Al Boum Photo, who became the first back-to-back winner of the Gold Cup since Best Mate won his third in 2004. Al Boum Photo was one of seven winners at the Cheltenham Festival for Ireland's perennial champion trainer Willie Mullins, who also won nearly a quarter of the Grade 1s in Britain and Ireland in the latest season, including seven of the 23 that were run in Ireland. That haul included the Dublin Chase at the Dublin Racing Festival won by Chacun Pour Soi, who was another high-profile absentee from the Queen Mother Champion Chase, sadly being ruled out on the morning of the race. The depleted field for that contest allowed Politologue the opportunity to bag a first Festival victory at the fifth attempt for Paul Nicholls, who still had every chance of retaining the trainers' championship at the time of racing's suspension. In the event, Nicky Henderson's four winners at the Cheltenham Festival—including a record eighth success in the Champion Hurdle with Epatante—ensured he had just enough in reserve to take the title for a sixth time.

Staying chasers

Appearances on a racecourse have been few and far between for **Al Boum Photo** (c171) over the last two seasons, but his unconventional route to Cheltenham is clearly one that works for him, once again arriving at the Festival in peak condition after winning a Grade 3 event at Tramore on New Year's Day. The latest renewal of the Gold Cup was an enthralling race to watch, with most of the field still in contention jumping three out, and the first four were covered by less than two lengths at the line, Al Boum Photo holding off the late thrust of **Santini** (c170) by a neck, with **Lostintranslation** (c168) and **Monalee** (c168) finishing hot on their heels in third and fourth, respectively. The winner is a top-class chaser (if not an outstanding one) and his terrific attitude should continue to stand him in good stead, still young enough to think a third Gold Cup win is a distinct possibility in 2021. Santini and Lostintranslation should also continue to take high rank in this division after their good runs in defeat, while similar comments apply to **Delta Work** (c168), who is better than he showed when only fifth at Cheltenham. He had previously established himself as one of the best staying chasers in Ireland by winning both the Savills Chase and Irish Gold Cup at Leopardstown, even if Monalee was arguably unlucky not to beat him in the first-named

Al Boum Photo (right) and Lostintranslation jump the last together in the Gold Cup

event (jockey Rachael Blackmore lost her irons in the last 50 yards). **Kemboy** (c167+) ended the 2018/19 campaign as Timeform's highest-rated staying chaser on either side of the Irish Sea, but he failed to match that form in three starts during the latest season, including when managing only seventh in the Gold Cup. **Clan des Obeaux** (c165) and **Bristol de Mai** (c167x) were others who finished down the field at Cheltenham, though both horses are clearly still capable of top-class form under the right conditions. The latter proved as much when filling the runner-up spot in both the Betfair Chase at Haydock (one and a half lengths behind Lostintranslation) and the Cotswold Chase at Cheltenham (three and a half lengths behind Santini), while Clan des Obeaux ran out an impressive winner of the King George at Kempton for the second year in a row, stepping up markedly on his reappearance behind **Road To Respect** (c166) in the Champion Chase at Down Royal. Road To Respect sadly missed the second half of the season due to injury, whilst perhaps the most significant absentee from the Gold Cup was the 2018 winner **Native River** (c168), who had looked back to something like his best before a setback also ruled him out of Cheltenham.

Two-mile chasers

Few horses in the history of National Hunt racing have compiled a CV to match that of **Altior** (c175+), the winner of 19 successive races over jumps, including back-to-back renewals of the Queen Mother Champion Chase at the Cheltenham Festival. However, his winning sequence finally came to an end when stepped up in trip for his first start of the latest season, ultimately finding **Cyrname** (c174) too strong in the 1965 Chase at Ascot, and he was then on the sidelines for three months before reappearing with a characteristically dominant display in the Game Spirit Chase at Newbury. That performance suggested he wasn't going to give up his Champion Chase crown without a fight, but he had forfeited favouritism by that stage to **Defi du Seuil** (c169), who had made the most of Altior's absence to dominate the division in Britain, reeling off a hat-trick of wins in the Shloer Chase at Cheltenham, Tingle Creek Chase at Sandown and Clarence House Chase at Ascot. Throw into the mix the leading Irish-trained contender **Chacun Pour Soi** (c176), who produced the best performance of the season on Timeform ratings when beating stablemate **Min** (c174) in the Dublin Chase at Leopardstown, and the Queen Mother Champion Chase was shaping up to be the race of the Cheltenham Festival. In the event, however, the highlight on the second day of the meeting proved to be a huge anti-climax, with Altior and Chacun Pour Soi both having to be withdrawn after suffering minor setbacks in the 48 hours before the race, while the only one of the big three left standing, Defi du Seuil, turned in a lacklustre effort as odds-on favourite. That left the path clear for **Politologue** (c168)—a top-class chaser but one whose limitations are well established—to finally get his head in front at the Festival, making all to beat stablemate **Dynamite Dollars** (c160+) by nine and a half lengths. Min followed his defeat to Chacun Pour Soi with a deserved first win of his own at the Cheltenham Festival, when beating **Saint Calvados** (c165) and **A Plus Tard** (c164+) in a top-class renewal of the Ryanair Chase. We were also treated to a rare appearance from stablemate **Douvan** (166+), who has been plagued by issues but showed he still retains plenty of ability when easily

Politologue runs out an impressive winner of the Champion Chase

winning the Clonmel Oil Chase, while it was time to say goodbye to another Mullins-trained superstar in **Un de Sceaux** (c168), who brought the curtain down on a glittering career after chasing home Defi du Seuil in the Clarence House.

Novice chasers

This division threw up some of the most exciting finishes of the Cheltenham Festival, with few races all season capable of matching the RSA Chase for pure drama. **Minella Indo** (c160p), who had won the Albert Bartlett at the meeting 12 months earlier, looked set for a second Festival success after edging ahead of old rival **Allaho** (158p) on the run-in, but the pair were remarkably pegged back by **Champ** (161p), who had been eight lengths down at the last but produced a surge up the run-in to get up close home and score by a length. Still relatively unexposed over staying trips, Champ certainly showed enough to suggest he will relish the longer trip of the Gold Cup, for which he must be considered a leading contender in 2021 if brushing up on his jumping. Minella Indo and Allaho also have the potential to develop into top-class chasers at around 3m, whereas up-and-comers in the 2m division are seemingly thin on the ground, the likes of **Notebook** (155)—who was unbeaten over fences before flopping in the Arkle Chase—having plenty to find to come up to the level of Chacun Pour Soi and co. **Put The Kettle On** (c147) was still a noteworthy winner of the Arkle in a historical context, repelling the persistent challenge of **Fakir d'Oudairies** (c154) to become the first mare to land the prize since Anaglogs Daughter in 1980. The Marsh Novices' Chase didn't exist back then, but there have already been some high-class renewals since its inception in 2011, including the latest one won by **Samcro** (c159). It was a fine training performance from Gordon Elliott given how many issues Samcro has had since also landing the Ballymore at the 2018 Cheltenham Festival, the eight-year-old looking back to something like his best as he dug deep to beat **Melon** (c158) by a nose. Another length back in third was **Faugheen** (c160), who was sent chasing at the age of 11 and showed himself still capable of high-class form, notably winning a Grade 1 at Limerick on Boxing Day that has since been renamed in his honour. Others who tasted success at Grade 1 level in this division included **Battleoverdoyen** (c151) and **tchy Feet** (c151p), while **Simply The Betts** (c154p), **Chosen Mate** (c153p) and **Imperial Aura** (c153p) all achieved notable ratings in winning Festival handicaps.

Staying hurdlers

The Stayers' Hurdle at the Cheltenham Festival was blown wide open by the unexpected misstep of defending champion **Paisley Park** (h161), with a bunch of upstart handicappers and exposed graded performers making up the bulk of those who featured in an unusually bunched finish, the first sextet covered by only eight lengths at the line. The winner **Lisnagar Oscar** (h158) clearly took a big step forward to beat the progressive Irish raider **Ronald Pump** (h156) by two lengths, but that success seems unlikely to signal a spell of dominance in the division. For context, **Sire du Berlais** (h159) produced more in pure form terms when winning the Pertemps Final for the second year in succession on the same card. Everything had gone smoothly for Paisley Park up to the Festival, running out a comfortable winner of both the Long Distance Hurdle at Newbury and Cleeve Hurdle at Cheltenham. He was found to be suffering from an irregular heartbeat after managing only seventh in the Stayers' Hurdle, so the run is probably best overlooked under the circumstances, and it would be no surprise were he to re-establish himself as very much the one to beat in this division in 2020/21. **The Worlds End** (h151) took advantage of Paisley's Park absence (withdrawn due to unsuitable going) to win a below-par renewal of the Long Walk Hurdle at Ascot, while **Emitom** (h152) and **Summerville Boy** (h156) also struck at graded level before finishing fourth and fifth, respectively, in the Stayers' Hurdle. Notable absentees from that race included **If The Cap Fits** (h159), who won the Ascot Hurdle on his reappearance, and **Benie des Dieux** (h159), who looked potentially the biggest danger to Paisley Park after her 21-length victory in the Galmoy Hurdle at Gowran Park but ended up running in the Mares' Hurdle at the Festival instead. She is clearly a very smart mare on her day and will be a match for any of the geldings in this division when given the chance to take them on, as was the case over the years with **Apple's Jade** (h150), who was retired after finishing down the field at Cheltenham. A credit to her connections, she'd lost a good bit in terms of ability and consistency during the latest season but did enjoy one last hurrah when recording the eleventh Grade 1 success of her career in the Frank Ward Memorial Hurdle at Leopardstown.

Two-mile hurdlers

Much of the talk before the Champion Hurdle revolved around it being a substandard edition, with **Epatante** (h161p) standing out as one of very few in the race still open to improvement. The form of her impressive success in the Christmas Hurdle at Kempton (by five lengths from **Silver Streak** (h154) was the best on offer, too, and she duly posted a

Epatante (centre) caps a brilliant season with victory in the Champion Hurdle

comfortable three-length victory to banish the memories of her disappointing display in the Mares' Novices' Hurdle 12 months earlier. When you factor in that she was receiving a 7 lb mares' allowance, then Epatante earned a rating as low as any Champion Hurdle winner this century, but she did score in smooth style so could be capable of achieving a higher figure under the right conditions. Irish-trained runners filled the next four places, with **Sharjah** (h163) emerging from the pack to take second ahead of **Darver Star** (h157), **Cilaos Emery** (h156) and **Petit Mouchoir** (h158). It was an in-and-out season for Sharjah, whose victory in the Matheson Hurdle at Leopardstown (for the second year in a row) was sandwiched between below-par performances in the Morgiana Hurdle at Punchestown and Irish Champion Hurdle back at Leopardstown. The Morgiana was won by stablemate **Saldier** (h156), who missed the rest of the season due to injury, while the Irish Champion was won in workmanlike fashion by **Honeysuckle** (h160), who didn't need to run to the same level as she had when landing the Hatton's Grace Hurdle at Fairyhouse on her previous start. Honeysuckle is now unbeaten in eight starts under Rules after also winning the Mares' Hurdle at the Cheltenham Festival, in which she improved again to foil Benie des Dieux in a thrilling contest. The performance she posted was good enough to suggest she would have given Epatante plenty to think about in the Champion Hurdle (for which she had been considered), while it's not impossible that she may yet have even more to offer, still only a six-year-old after all. The most significant absentee from this division was the dual Champion Hurdle winner **Buveur d'Air** (h155+), who suffered an injury when failing to peg back the enterprisingly-ridden **Cornerstone Lad** (h150) in the Fighting Fifth Hurdle at Newcastle and missed the rest of the season as a result. He's still only nine and will hopefully be back to try and regain his Champion Hurdle crown in 2021, though stablemate Epatante will clearly provide stern opposition.

Novice hurdlers

The winners of the three Grade 1 novice hurdles at the Cheltenham Festival each have plenty to recommend them for the future, not least **Envoi Allen** (160p), who extended his winning sequence under Rules to eight when recording a dominant success in the Ballymore Novices' Hurdle. His performance was everything his record had promised, confirming himself a top-class prospect in the way that he first closed down the pair who had dominated, **Easywork** (h149) and **The Big Getaway** (h148p), and then went away from them in authoritative fashion. He's now set to go novice chasing and will surely take high rank in that division. Similar comments apply to **Shishkin** (159p), who went unbeaten in three completed starts over hurdles, culminating with a gutsy success in the Supreme Novices' Hurdle at Cheltenham. He enjoyed a less-than-ideal trip through the race but stuck to his task well to overhaul the smooth-travelling **Abacadabras** (h158) in a thrilling battle after the final flight. The runner-up ran a cracker and appeals as a likely contender for the 2021 Champion Hurdle, while **Chantry House** (h144) shaped encouragingly in third and, like Shiskin, he is included in our Fifty as a smart prospect for novice chasing. Back in fourth was the favourite **Asterion Forlonge** (h150), who had been impressive when winning a Grade 1 at Leopardstown on his previous start but hampered his chance (and others) at Cheltenham by jumping markedly right. That was just the first act in what was a frustrating start to the week for trainer Willie Mullins, but his luck had soon turned by Friday, when he won the first four races on the card. **Burning Victory** (h140p) got the ball rolling in the Triumph Hurdle, though it's fair to say that she was a fortunate winner, almost certain to have been second best if **Goshen** (h161p) had negotiated the last safely. Goshen was around 10 lengths clear when unseating Jamie Moore at that flight and would have been a well above-average winner of the Triumph, so it will be no surprise if he is targeted at the Champion Hurdle in 2020/21. That comment also applies to **Saint Roi** (h150p), who made a mockery of his opening mark when winning the County Hurdle, while Mullins' other winner on Friday before Al Boum Photo's Gold Cup success came in the shape of **Monkfish** (h150p). He defied a big step up in class to land a closely-contested renewal of the Albert Bartlett Novices' Hurdle, showing a game attitude to repel **Latest Exhibition** (h149), **Fury Road** (h149) and **Thyme Hill** (h149) in a bunched finish. That is likely to prove a typically informative contest, especially with a view to chasing, Monkfish certainly having the physique to suggest he is a smashing prospect for a race like the RSA in 2020/21.

2019/20 STATISTICS (Britain)

TRAINERS (1,2,3 earnings)		Horses	Indiv'l Wnrs	Races Won	Runs	% Strike Rate	Stakes £
1	Nicky Henderson	169	76	118	456	25.9	2,452,176
2	Paul Nicholls	150	69	96	445	21.6	2,270,994
3	Dan Skelton	212	76	119	724	16.4	1,410,892
4	W. P. Mullins, Ireland	63	8	8	68	11.8	1,341,527
5	Nigel Twiston-Davies	118	47	71	433	16.4	1,252,541
6	Colin Tizzard	107	41	61	407	15.0	1,189,537
7	Philip Hobbs	128	47	75	419	17.9	1,065,272
8	Gordon Elliott, Ireland	92	20	28	126	22.2	788,627
9	David Pipe	87	43	64	341	18.8	700,600
10	Olly Murphy	112	48	67	351	19.1	589,278

JOCKEYS (by winners)		1st	2nd	3rd	Unpl	Total Rides	% Strike Rate
1	Brian Hughes	141	102	101	370	714	19.7
2	Richard Johnson	122	104	112	331	669	18.2
3	Sam Twiston-Davies	99	83	90	318	590	16.8
4	Harry Skelton	97	88	67	220	472	20.6
5	Harry Cobden	83	66	52	198	399	20.8
6	Aidan Coleman	82	62	51	222	417	19.7
7	Nico de Boinville	73	54	30	161	318	23.0
8	Gavin Sheehan	70	47	42	195	354	19.8
9	Adam Wedge	65	52	52	289	458	14.2
10	Jonjo O'Neill Jr.	61	45	47	195	348	17.5

SIRES OF WINNERS (1,2,3 earnings)		Races Won	Runs	% Strike Rate	Stakes £
1	Milan (by Sadler's Wells)	69	556	12.4	1,030,793
2	King's Theatre (by Sadler's Wells)	56	338	16.6	1,026,053
3	Stowaway (by Slip Anchor)	59	481	12.3	902,341
4	Oscar (by Sadler's Wells)	54	497	10.9	819,990
5	Westerner (by Danehill)	52	461	11.3	813,011
6	Beneficial (by Top Ville)	57	407	14.0	791,447
7	Flemensfirth (by Alleged)	50	457	10.9	782,051
8	Kayf Tara (by Sadler's Wells)	60	456	13.2	705,475
9	Yeats (by Sadler's Wells)	55	466	11.8	698,134
10	Gold Well (by Sadler's Wells)	69	438	15.8	689,418

LEADING HORSES (1,2,3 earnings)		Races Won	Runs	Stakes £
1	Epatante 6 b.f No Risk At All–Kadjara	3	3	367,120
2	Al Boum Photo 8 b.g Buck's Boum–Al Gane	1	1	351,688
3	Politologue 9 gr.g Poliglote–Scarlet Row	1	3	250,300
4	Defi du Seuil 7 b.g Voix du Nord–Quarvine du Seuil	3	4	217,785
5	Santini 8 b.g Milan–Tinagoodnight	2	3	212,051
6	Lostintranslation 8 b.g Flemensfirth–Falika	2	4	207,123
7	Min 9 b.g Walk In The Park–Phemyka	1	1	198,135
8	Lisnagar Oscar 7 b.g Oscar–Asta Belle	1	6	193,117
9	Riders Onthe Storm 7 br.g Scorpion–Endless Moment	3	4	178,247
10	The Conditional 8 b.g Kalanisi–Gorrie Vale	2	5	153,260

SECTION 5

THE TIMEFORM TOP 100

Hurdlers

Rating	Horse
163	Sharjah
161p	Epatante (f)
161p	Goshen
161	Paisley Park
160p	Envoi Allen
160	Honeysuckle (f)
159p	Shishkin
159	Benie des Dieux (f)
159	If The Cap Fits
159	Sire du Berlais
158	Abacadabras
158	Lisnagar Oscar
157	Darver Star
156	Bapaume
156	Cilaos Emery
156	Mr Adjudicator
156	Ronald Pump
156	Saldier
156	Summerville Boy
155+	Buveur d'Air
155	Bacardys
155	Petit Mouchoir
155	The Storyteller
154	Silver Streak
153	Burrows Saint
153	Klassical Dream
153	William Henry
152	Cracking Smart
152	Emitom
152	Le Prezien
152	Pentland Hills
152	Thistlecrack
152	Wicklow Brave
151	Call Me Lord
151	Charli Parcs
151	Elfile (f)
151	Kilfenora
151	The Worlds End
151	Vision des Flos
150p	Monkfish
150p	Saint Roi
150+	Supasundae
150	Apple's Jade (f)
150	Asterion Forlonge
150	Cornerstone Lad
150	Darasso
150	Thomas Darby
149	Aramon
149	Ballyandy
149	Brain Power
149	Davids Charm
149	Easywork
149	Fury Road
149	Latest Exhibition
149	Quel Destin
149	Roksana (f)
149	Sole Pretender
149	Thyme Hill
149	Tobefair
149§	L'Ami Serge
148p	Dame de Compagnie (f)
148p	The Big Getaway
148	Band of Outlaws
148	Ch'tibello
148	Monsieur Lecoq
148	Pic d'Orhy
148	Stormy Ireland (f)
147	Agrapart
147	Black Tears (f)
147	Coeur Sublime
147	Indefatigable (f)
147	Janika
147	Jetz
147	Song For Someone
147	Tudor City
147	Unowhatimeanharry
146p	Allmankind
146	Bachasson
146	Concertista (f)
146	Eglantine du Seuil (f)
146	Fusil Raffles
146	Gumball
146	Penhill
145	Aspire Tower
145	Column of Fire
145	Embittered
145	Janidil
145	Le Patriote
145	Main Fact
145	Saglawy
144+	Diego du Charmil
144	Canardier
144	Chantry House
144	Eldorado Allen
144	Grand Sancy
144	Itchy Feet
144	Jatiluwih
144	Mt Leinster
144	The Jam Man
143	Aux Ptits Soins
143	Birchdale
143	Edwardstone
143	Killultagh Vic
143	Magic of Light (f)
143	Sayo
143	Sporting John
143	Stratum
143	Top Notch
143	Turnpike Trip

Chasers

Rating	Horse
176p	Chacun Pour Soi
175+	Altior
174	Cyrname
174	Min
171	Al Boum Photo
170	Santini
169	Defi du Seuil
168	Delta Work
168	Lostintranslation
168	Monalee
168	Native River
168	Politologue
168	Tiger Roll
168	Un de Sceaux
167+	Kemboy
167	Waiting Patiently
167x	Bristol de Mai
166+	Cilaos Emery
166+	Douvan
166	Road To Respect
165	Ballyoisin
165	Clan des Obeaux
165	Presenting Percy
165	Saint Calvados
164+	A Plus Tard
164	Real Steel
163+	Riders Onthe Storm
163	Vinndication
162	Black Corton
162	Chris's Dream
161p	Champ
161	Definitly Red
161	Elegant Escape
161	Janika
160p	Minella Indo
160	Ballyoptic
160	Faugheen
160	Footpad
160	Hardline
159+	Samcro
159	Alpha des Obeaux
159	Bachasson
159	Dolos
159	Jett
159	Kalashnikov
159	Sceau Royal
159	Top Ville Ben
159§	Beware The Bear
158p	Allaho
158p	Easysland
158	Duc des Genievres
158	Frodon
158	Melon
158	Simply Ned
157	Acapella Bourgeois
157	Bun Doran
157	Cepage
157	Total Recall
157	Yala Enki
156	Castlegrace Paddy
156	Peregrine Run
156	Voix du Reve
155	Brave Eagle
155	De Rasher Counter
155	Diego du Charmil
155	Dynamite Dollars
155	Lalor
155	Notebook
154p	Simply The Betts
154	Easy Game

154 Fakir d'Oudairies
154 Forest Bihan
154 Kildisart
154 Secret Investor
154 Snow Falcon
153p Chosen Mate
153p Glen Forsa
153p Imperial Aura
153 Aso
153 Kimberlite Candy
153 Lady Buttons (f)
153 Magic Saint
153 Mister Fisher
153 Mister Whitaker
153 Ok Corral
153 Siruh du Lac
153 Tout Est Permis
152 Eclair de Beaufeu
152 Happy Diva (f)
152 Walk In The Mill
151p Itchy Feet
151 Battleoverdoyen
151 Bellshill
151 Cash Back
151 Crievehill
151 Mister Malarky
151 Nuts Well
151 Ornua
151 Spiritofthegames
151 Traffic Fluide
151x Keeper Hill
151x Keeper Hill
152 Otago Trail
152 Ramses de Teillee
152 Robinsfirth

Juvenile Hurdlers

161p Goshen
146p Allmankind
145 Aspire Tower
141 A Wave of The Sea
141 Aramax
141 Navajo Pass
140p Burning Victory (f)
140 Sir Psycho
140 Wolf Prince
139p Botox Has
139 Cerberus
139 Solo
138 Nordano
137 Mick Pastor
132p Grand Roi
132 Night Edition
130 Fujimoto Flyer (f)
130 Never Do Nothing
129 Clemencia
129 Langer Dan
128 Saint d'Oroux
126 Blacko
126 Extreme Force
126 Midnights' Gift (f)
126 Monte Cristo
126 Palladium
126 Recent Revelations
126 Tavus
125p Rowland Ward
125 Stratagem

Novice Hurdlers

160p Envoi Allen
159p Shishkin
158 Abacadabras
150p Monkfish
150p Saint Roi
150 Asterion Forlonge
149 Easywork
149 Fury Road
149 Latest Exhibition
149 Thyme Hill
148p The Big Getaway
146 Concertista (f)
145 Column of Fire
145 Embittered
145 Janidil
144 Chantry House
144 Mt Leinster
143 Edwardstone
143 Sporting John
143 Turnpike Trip
142p Five O'Clock
142p Mcfabulous
142 Fiddlerontheroof
142 Master Debonair
142 The Cashel Man
141p Cedarwood Road
141 Sebastopol
141 Top Moon
140 Alfa Mix
140 Beacon Edge

Novice Chasers

161p Champ
160p Minella Indo
160 Faugheen
159+ Samcro
158p Allaho
158 Melon
155 Notebook
154p Simply The Betts
154 Easy Game
154 Fakir d'Oudairies
153p Chosen Mate
153p Imperial Aura
153 Mister Fisher
152 Eclair de Beaufeu
151p Itchy Feet
151 Battleoverdoyen
151 Cash Back
150p Greaneteen
150 Champagne Classic
150 Global Citizen
150 Ravenhill
150 Slate House
149 Al Dancer
149 Copperhead
149 Lord du Mesnil
149 Rouge Vif
149 Truckers Lodge
148 Black Op
148 First Flow
148 Tornado Flyer

NH Flat Horses

123 Ferny Hollow
119 Appreciate It
118 Easy As That
114 Eskylane
114 Third Time Lucki
112 Ask A Honey Bee
111 Adrimel
111 Queens Brook (f)
111 Tupelo Mississippi
110 Israel Champ
110 Red Rookie
109 Eric Bloodaxe
109 Forged In Fire
108 Darling Daughter (f)
107P Bob Olinger
107 Champagnesuperover
107 Tactical Move
107 Your Darling
106p Flinteur Sacre
106 Nada To Prada (f)
106 Smurphy Enki
106 Wide Receiver
105p Captain Kangaroo
105p Farouk d'Alene
105p Mont Segur
105 Bear Ghylls
105 Coquelicot (f)
105 Fire Attack
105 Idas Boy
105 Julies Stowaway
105 Step To The Top (f)

Hunter Chasers

139 Captain Cattistock
137 Asockastar
137 Hazel Hill
136 It Came To Pass
135 Risk A Fine
135 Shantou Flyer
134 Killaro Boy
134x Minella Rocco
133p Billaway
133 Bob And Co
132p Aloneamongmillions
132 Alcala
132 Wishing And Hoping
131 Monsieur Gibraltar
130 Bishops Road
130 Caryto des Brosses
130 Chef d'Equipe
130 Virak
129+ Staker Wallace
129 More Buck's
128 Dylrow
128 Southfield Vic
127 The Dellercheckout
126 Swift Crusador
125 Dieu Vivant
124+ Monbeg Gold
124 Ballotin
124§ Mustmeetalady
123 Clondaw Westie

PROMISING HORSES

A p symbol is used by Timeform to denote horses we believe are capable of improvement, with a P symbol suggesting a horse is capable of much better form. Below is a list of selected British and Irish-trained horses with a p or P, listed under their current trainers.

PETER ATKINSON
Irish Roe (Ire) 9 b.m ... h130 c117p

CAROLINE BAILEY
Boldmere 7 b.g ... c143p

KIM BAILEY
Does He Know 5 b.g ... h123p
Imperial Aura (Ire) 7 b.g ... h132p c153p
Shanacoole Prince (Ire) 7 ch.g ... h116p

GILLIAN BOANAS
Crixus's Escape (Ire) 7 ch.g ... h117 c131p

MARTIN BRASSIL, IRELAND
City Island (Ire) 7 b.g ... h135 c117p

DAVID BRIDGWATER
Enrichissant (Fr) 6 b. or br.g ... c126p

HENRY DE BROMHEAD, IRELAND
Captain Guinness (Ire) 5 b.g ... h137p
Minella Indo (Ire) 7 b.g ... c160p
Spyglass Hill (Ire) 7 b.g ... h125 c138p

CHARLES BYRNES, IRELAND
Off You Go (Ire) 7 b.g ... h125 c132p

MICK CHANNON
Glen Forsa (Ire) 8 b.g ... c153p

DAVID CHRISTIE, IRELAND
Winged Leader (Ire) 6 b.g ... c118p

DAVID COTTIN, FRANCE
Easysland (Fr) 6 b. or br.g ... c158p

S. CURLING, IRELAND
Aloneamongmillions (Ire) 7 b.g ... c132p

KEITH DALGLEISH
First Account 6 b. or br.g ... h124 c124p
Newtown Boy (Ire) 7 b.g ... h123 c97p
Prince Kayf 6 b.g ... h125p

HENRY DALY
It's Probably Me 5 b.m ... h122p b95

MISS ELIZABETH DOYLE, IRELAND
Cayd Boy (Fr) 5 b.g ... h132p

MICHAEL EASTERBY
Albert's Back 6 b.g ... c127p

STUART EDMUNDS
Rowland Ward 4 b.g ... h125p

GORDON ELLIOTT, IRELAND
Chosen Mate (Ire) 7 br.g ... h137 c153p
Count Simon (Ire) 6 b.g ... h129 c126p
Daylight Katie (Fr) 7 b.m ... h130p
Envoi Allen (Fr) 6 b.g ... h160p
Galvin (Ire) 6 b.g ... c146p
Glenloe (Ire) 9 br.g ... c132p
Milan Native (Ire) 7 br.g ... h109 c146p
Miss Aloud (Ire) 6 br.m ... h121p b87
The Bosses Oscar (Ire) 5 b.g ... h136p b94
Tronador (Ire) 4 ch.g ... h121p

BRIAN ELLISON
Weakfield (Ire) 7 b.g ... c128p

JAMES EWART
Sao Maxence (Fr) 7 b.g ... h116p

JOHNNY FARRELLY
Addis Ababa (Ire) 5 ch.g ... h115p

PHILIP FENTON, IRELAND
Groody Rover (Ire) 6 b.g ... h132p

HARRY FRY
Ask Me Early (Ire) 6 gr.g ... h116p
King Roland (Ire) 6 br.g ... h135p
Phoenix Way (Ire) 7 b.g ... h141p
Samarquand 6 b.g ... c131p
Winningseverything (Ire) 6 b.g ... h133p

TOM GEORGE
Big Bresil 5 b.g ... h123p b89
Come On Teddy (Ire) 6 b.g ... h126p
Hooligan (Ire) 5 b.g ... h122p b80
Summerville Boy (Ire) 8 b.g ... h156 c143p

CHRIS GORDON
Highway One O Two (Ire) 5 b. or br.g ... h139p b88

MRS J. HARRINGTON, IRELAND
Gin On Lime (Fr) 4 b.f ... h121p
Silver Sheen 6 b.g ... h136p

NICKY HENDERSON
Angels Breath (Ire) 6 gr.g ... c148p
Birchdale (Ire) 6 b.g ... h143 c108p
Bond's Lover (Ire) 6 gr.m ... h117p
Burrows Edge (Fr) 7 b.g ... h136 c137p
Caribean Boy (Fr) 6 gr.g ... c146p
Champ (Ire) 8 b.g ... c161p
Champagne Platinum (Ire) 6 gr.g ... h122 c133p
Craigneiche (Ire) 6 br.g ... h119p b101
Dame de Compagnie (Fr) 7 b.m ... h148p
Daphne du Clos (Fr) 7 b.m ... h121p
Diablo de Rouhet (Fr) 7 b.g ... h143p c145
Epatante (Fr) 6 b.m ... h161p
Fix Sun (Fr) 5 b.g ... h125p
Glynn (Ire) 6 b.g ... h129p
Grand Roi (Fr) 4 b.g ... h132p b103
Marie's Rock (Ire) 5 b. or br.m ... h140P b94p
Mister Coffey (Fr) 5 b.g ... h127p
Pipesmoker (Fr) 5 b.g ... h125p b78
Shishkin (Ire) 6 b.g ... h159p
Timberman (Ire) 5 b.g ... h119P b97p
Time Flies By (Ire) 5 ch.g ... h120p b103

PHILIP HOBBS
Espion (Fr) 6 ch.g ... h122p
Evidence de Thaix (Fr) 6 b.m ... c132p
Kalooki (Ger) 6 b.g ... h131p
Masters Legacy (Ire) 5 br.g ... h126p
Musical Slave (Ire) 7 b.g ... c139p
Pileon (Ire) 6 b.g ... h140p
Potters Venture (Ire) 6 b.g ... h126p
Raven Court (Ire) 6 b.g ... h115p
St Barts (Ire) 6 b.g ... h126p

DENIS HOGAN, IRELAND
Macgiloney (Ire) 7 b.g ... h128 c125p

ANTHONY HONEYBALL
Gustavian (Ire) 5 b.g ... h116p b100
Kid Commando 6 b.g ... h129p b102
Kilconny Bridge (Ire) 6 b.m ... h123p b92
Wagner (Ire) 5 b.g ... h116p

RUTH JEFFERSON
Buster Valentine (Ire) 7 b.g ... c133p
Clondaw Caitlin (Ire) 5 b.m ... h130p b94
Mega Yeats (Ire) 6 br.m ... h125p

D. J. JEFFREYS
Petrastar 5 b.g ... h119p

SAM JUKES
Marcle Ridge (Ire) 8 b.g ... c115p

DAVID KEMP
Law of Gold (Ire) 7 b.g ... c115p

ALAN KING
Fraternel (Fr) 5 b.g ... h116p
Isolate (Fr) 4 b.g ... h118p
Lisp (Ire) 6 ch.g ... h139 c141p
On To Victory 6 b.g ... h121p
Passing Call 7 b.m ... h119 c117p
Temple High 5 b.m ... h115p

PHILIP KIRBY
Show Promise 6 b.g ... h123p b88

TOM LACEY
Lamanver Storm 5 b.g ... h122p b82

JUSTIN LANDY
Shetland Bus (Ger) 7 ch.g ... h115 c105p

EMMA LAVELLE
Doc Penfro 8 b.g ... h134p
Fedelta (Ire) 6 b.g ... h117p
Manofthemountain (Ire) 7 b.g ... c127p
The Domino Effect (Ire) 6 b.g ... h115p

CHARLIE LONGSDON

Do Wanna Know (Ire) 6 b.g. h122p
Illegal Model (Ire) 6 b.g. h118p

DONALD MCCAIN

Gaelik Coast (Fr) 6 br.g. h125p

JOHN MCCONNELL, IRELAND

Construct 5 b.g. h124p

OLIVER MCKIERNAN, IRELAND

Unexpected Depth (Ire) 6 b.g. h133p

GRAEME MCPHERSON

Ask Henry (Ire) 7 b.g. h118p b87

NOEL MEADE, IRELAND

Diol Ker (Fr) 6 b.g. h135p
School Boy Hours (Ire) 7 b.g. c132p

A. L. T. MOORE, IRELAND

Sea Ducor 4 b.g. h121p

GARY MOORE

Botox Has (Fr) 4 b.g. h139p
Esprit de Somoza (Fr) 6 b.g. c119p
Goshen (Fr) 4 b.g. h161p

NEIL MULHOLLAND

La Cavsa Nostra (Ire) 8 b.g. c122p
Rookie Trainer (Ire) 6 b.g. h116p

EMMET MULLINS, IRELAND

Zero Ten (Ire) 7 b.g. c143p

W. P. MULLINS, IRELAND

Allaho (Fr) 6 b.g. h138 c158p
Annamix (Fr) 7 gr.g. h116 c140p
Billaway (Ire) 8 b.g. c133p
Blackbow (Ire) 7 b.g. h127p
Breaken (Fr) 6 b.g. h128 c138p
Burning Victory (Fr) 4 br.f. h140p
Canardier (Fr) 8 b.g. h144 c135p
Contingency 7 b.m. h126 c135p
Elimay (Fr) 6 gr.m. h137 c141p
Energumene (Fr) 6 br.g. h138p b98
Five O'Clock (Fr) 5 b.g. h142p
Francin (Fr) 7 b.g. h133p
Lord Royal (Fr) 5 gr.g. h135p
Monkfish (Ire) 6 ch.g. h150p
Saint Roi (Fr) 5 br.g. h150p
Salsaretta (Fr) 7 b.m. c144p

COLM A. MURPHY, IRELAND

Relegate (Ire) 7 b.m. h134p

OLLY MURPHY

Brewin'upastorm (Ire) 7 b.g. c148p
Collooney (Ire) 6 b.g. h125p
Endlessly (Ire) 5 b.g. h119p
Enemy Coast Ahead 6 br.g. h121p
Finawn Bawn (Ire) 7 b.g. c121p
Itchy Feet (Fr) 6 b.g. h144 c151p
Presence of Mind (Ire) 5 b.g. h118p b99
Seemingly So (Ire) 7 br.g. h100 c119p
Timeforaspin 6 b.g. h115p

JAMES A. NASH, IRELAND

Alohamora (Ire) 6 ch.m. h120 c124p

DR RICHARD NEWLAND

Forecast 8 ch.g. h132 c116p
Mr Muldoon (Ire) 7 ch.g. h128p
Rostello (Fr) 5 ch.g. h117 c100p

PAUL NICHOLLS

Ask For Glory (Ire) 6 b.g. h125p
Cap du Mathan (Fr) 5 b.g. h120p
Cill Anna (Ire) 5 b.m. h132p b83
Danny Whizzbang (Ire) 7 b.g. c144p
Diamond Guy (Fr) 7 b.g. h121p
Fidelio Vallis (Fr) 5 b.g. h128p
Getaway Trump (Ire) 7 b.g. c140p
Greaneteen (Fr) 6 b.g. c150p
Highland Hunter (Ire) 7 gr.g. h130p
Malaya (Fr) 6 b.m. h131 c118p
Mcfabulous (Ire) 6 b.g. h142p
Mont des Avaloirs (Fr) 7 b.g. c141p
Posh Trish (Ire) 7 b.m. c124p
Red Risk (Fr) 5 b.g. c142p
Saint Sonnet (Fr) 5 b.g. h138 c142p
Soldier of Love 7 b.g. c118p
Southfield Harvest 6 b.g. h123p
Thyme White (Fr) 4 b.g. h124p
Topofthegame c162p

FERGAL O'BRIEN

Global Fame (Ire) 6 b.g. h118p b97
Imperial Alcazar (Ire) 6 b.g. h138p
Lough Har (Ire) 6 b.g. h101 c116p b80
Silver Hallmark 6 br. or gr.g. h119p

JOSEPH PATRICK O'BRIEN, IRELAND

Cut Em Down (Ire) 7 b.g. c132p
Front View (Fr) 5 gr.g. h133p b101
The Moyglass Flyer (Ire) 6 b.g. h131p
Thermistocles (Ire) 8 b.g. c130p
Uhtred (Ire) 5 b.g. h128p b108

GEAROID O'LOUGHLIN, IRELAND

Cedarwood Road (Ire) 5 b.g. h141p b74

DANNI O'NEILL

Tales of The Tweed (Ire) 8 b.g. c129p

JONJO O'NEILL

Arrivederci (Fr) 5 gr.g. h128p
Ashfield Paddy (Ire) 6 b.g. h126p
Bean In Trouble 6 gr.g. h126p
Carys' Commodity 5 b.g. h123p b94
Flight Deck (Ire) 6 b.g. h119p
Kilbrook (Ire) 5 b.g. h115p b98
Lunar Baby (Ire) 5 b.m. h119p
Palmers Hill (Ire) 7 b.g. h134p

RICHARD PHILLIPS

Iron Horse 9 b.g. h120 c99p

ELLA PICKARD

Getaround (Ire) 5 gr.g. h124p b98

DAVID PIPE

Brinkley (Fr) 5 gr.g. h135p b75

CHARLES & ADAM POGSON

Doux Pretender (Fr) 7 b.g. c124p

DECLAN QUEALLY, IRELAND

Western Victory (Ire) 7 b.m. h135 c118p

ALASTAIR RALPH

Billingsley (Ire) 8 b.g. c133p
Encounter A Giant (Ire) 8 b.g. c138p
Your Band 5 b.g. h117p

NICKY RICHARDS

Big Bad Bear (Ire) 6 br.g. h128p
Marown (Ire) 6 b.g. h132p

PAULINE ROBSON

Martila (Fr) 8 b.m. h117 c112p

JEREMY SCOTT

Dashel Drasher 7 b.g. c140p

MICHAEL SCUDAMORE

Do Your Job (Ire) 6 b.g. h119p

OLIVER SHERWOOD

Southern Sam 6 b.g. h109 c122p
Tarada 7 br.g. c139p
What's Occurring (Ire) 7 b.g. c123p

DAN SKELTON

Allmankind 4 b.g. h146p
Bennys King (Ire) 9 b.g. c149p
Floki 6 b.g. h119p
Vision du Puy (Fr) 5 b.m. h127p

SUE SMITH

Blaster Yeats 5 b.g. h102p
Captain Moirette (Fr) 8 gr.g. h130 c119p

JAMIE SNOWDEN

Legends Ryde 5 ch.m. h117p b100

SAM THOMAS

Iwilldoit 7 b.g. h108 c131p

SANDY THOMSON

Duc de Grissay (Fr) 7 b.g. h112 c119p

COLIN TIZZARD

Born In Borris (Ire) 6 b.m. h116p
Honest Exchange (Ire) 6 b.g. h118p
Jaytrack Parkhomes 6 b.g. h115 c117p
The Big Breakaway (Ire) 5 ch.g. h137p

NIGEL TWISTON-DAVIES

Kingofthecotswolds (Ire) 6 b.g. h109 c121p
Muckamore (Ire) 6 b.g. h122p
Sir Valentine (Ger) 7 b.g. h131p
Wholestone (Ire) 9 br.g. c145p

TIM VAUGHAN

Let The Heirs Walk (Ire) 6 b.g. h121p

ALISTAIR WHILLANS

Cracking Destiny (Ire) 7 b.g. h120p c131

HARRY WHITTINGTON

Simply The Betts (Ire) 7 b.g. c154p
Young Bull (Ire) 6 b.g. h130p

EVAN WILLIAMS

Fado des Brosses (Fr) 5 b.g. h129p
Imperial Flem (Ire) 5 b.g. h116p
Secret Reprieve (Ire) 6 b.g. c131p

IAN WILLIAMS

Blue Laureate 5 b.g. h125p
Seven de Baune (Fr) 7 ch.g. h118 c128p
The Grand Visir 6 b.g. h120p

MRS JANE WILLIAMS

Galice Macalo (Fr) 4 b.f. h116p

VENETIA WILLIAMS

Destinee Royale (Fr) 7 b.m. h107 c124p
Farrants Way (Ire) 6 b.g. h123p
Ibleo (Fr) 7 b.g. c134p
Lisa de Vassy (Fr) 5 b.m. h117p

TRAINERS FOR COURSES

The following statistics show the most successful trainers over the past five seasons at each of the courses that stage National Hunt racing in England, Scotland and Wales. Impact Value is expressed as a factor of a trainer's number of winners compared to those expected to occur by chance. Market Value is expressed as the factor by which the % chance of an Industry Starting Price exceeds random, as implied by field size. For example, a horse that is shorter than 3/1 in a 4-runner field will have a Market Value above 1.

AINTREE

Trainer	Wins	Runs	Strike Rate	% Rivals Beaten	P/L	Run To Form %	Impact Value	Market Value
Nicky Henderson	25	117	21.37%	58.31	1.30	58.97	1.98	1.74
Dan Skelton	18	123	14.63%	59.61	-7.56	68.29	1.25	1.48
Colin Tizzard	14	65	21.54%	59.55	84.32	58.46	2.21	1.46
Paul Nicholls	12	118	10.17%	52.45	-51.00	50.85	1.07	1.66
Nigel Twiston-Davies	11	98	11.22%	51.25	-38.00	53.57	1.19	1.56
W. P. Mullins, Ireland	10	54	18.52%	58.41	-3.15	64.81	2.11	2.08
Tom George	9	73	12.33%	52.00	4.00	50.68	1.32	1.29
Jonjo O'Neill	8	69	11.59%	45.55	-14.71	47.10	1.21	1.47
Harry Fry	7	41	17.07%	57.56	-5.27	63.41	1.50	1.61
Alan King	7	50	14.00%	56.13	-15.88	64.00	1.45	1.57

ASCOT

Trainer	Wins	Runs	Strike Rate	% Rivals Beaten	P/L	Run To Form %	Impact Value	Market Value
Nicky Henderson	32	158	20.25%	59.85	-9.39	70.57	1.61	1.91
Paul Nicholls	32	186	17.20%	56.64	-6.81	65.59	1.34	1.52
Harry Fry	14	66	21.21%	60.51	-0.26	69.70	1.91	1.71
Philip Hobbs	12	90	13.33%	56.56	-12.99	65.00	1.14	1.33
Alan King	10	84	11.90%	57.74	-40.71	68.45	1.14	1.53
Nigel Twiston-Davies	9	66	13.64%	49.93	-4.75	59.09	1.16	1.24
Gary Moore	9	93	9.68%	42.43	-33.30	44.09	0.83	0.89
Colin Tizzard	8	74	10.81%	48.92	-33.96	60.14	0.85	1.07
Dr Richard Newland	7	31	22.58%	60.43	27.25	66.13	2.07	1.18
David Pipe	7	45	15.56%	60.65	10.50	55.56	1.57	1.06

AYR

Trainer	Wins	Runs	Strike Rate	% Rivals Beaten	P/L	Run To Form %	Impact Value	Market Value
Nicky Richards	38	179	21.23%	61.46	-23.26	62.57	1.68	1.94
Lucinda Russell	29	252	11.51%	52.83	-89.74	54.76	0.89	1.08
N. W. Alexander	29	231	12.55%	51.90	-46.73	53.68	1.03	1.03
Iain Jardine	14	76	18.42%	53.16	1.98	50.66	1.51	1.21
Dan Skelton	14	48	29.17%	67.67	7.07	67.71	2.34	1.88
Stuart Crawford, Ireland	13	116	11.21%	49.04	-41.88	57.33	0.89	1.16
Sandy Thomson	12	76	15.79%	58.13	-29.58	57.89	1.38	1.52
Donald McCain	12	73	16.44%	45.84	-31.31	49.32	1.16	1.31
Gordon Elliott, Ireland	11	54	20.37%	67.01	-21.53	72.22	1.57	2.24
Ian Duncan	11	118	9.32%	48.12	-32.25	48.31	0.75	0.75

BANGOR-ON-DEE

Trainer	Wins	Runs	Strike Rate	% Rivals Beaten	P/L	Run To Form %	Impact Value	Market Value
Donald McCain	64	311	20.58%	59.13	47.70	59.16	1.52	1.30
Dan Skelton	27	114	23.68%	59.46	-10.32	60.53	1.94	1.96
Alan King	17	59	28.81%	69.80	-2.47	72.03	2.02	2.29
Jennie Candlish	14	78	17.95%	56.68	-11.45	55.77	1.53	1.21
Warren Greatrex	12	45	26.67%	59.67	5.54	54.44	1.99	1.96
Henry Daly	12	50	24.00%	60.73	42.75	59.00	1.98	1.20
Jonjo O'Neill	11	83	13.25%	48.83	-14.83	54.82	1.06	1.24
Nigel Twiston-Davies	11	72	15.28%	57.03	-22.23	57.64	1.17	1.58
Nicky Henderson	9	47	19.15%	55.50	-27.30	58.51	1.38	2.33
Gary Hanmer	8	45	17.78%	48.64	40.00	46.67	1.32	0.76

CARLISLE

Trainer	Wins	Runs	Strike Rate	% Rivals Beaten	P/L	Run To Form %	Impact Value	Market Value
Nicky Richards	23	86	26.74%	59.58	47.69	60.47	1.90	1.45
Donald McCain	22	192	11.46%	56.01	-64.92	58.33	0.85	1.28
Sue Smith	18	119	15.13%	51.54	-29.09	51.68	1.18	1.23
Stuart Crawford, Ireland	13	43	30.23%	68.19	4.32	72.09	2.20	1.73
Brian Ellison	13	51	25.49%	61.62	16.16	62.75	2.22	1.74
Micky Hammond	12	132	9.09%	40.05	-42.60	37.50	0.68	0.80
Lucinda Russell	10	135	7.41%	48.18	-28.25	44.81	0.64	1.04
Nigel Twiston-Davies	9	34	26.47%	62.70	0.92	69.12	1.98	2.46
Maurice Barnes	8	52	15.38%	50.97	18.50	51.92	1.27	0.69
Sandy Thomson	8	44	18.18%	47.62	14.85	48.86	1.29	1.25

CARTMEL

Trainer	Wins	Runs	Strike Rate	% Rivals Beaten	P/L	Run To Form %	Impact Value	Market Value
James Moffatt	26	233	11.16%	49.59	-12.47	43.99	0.90	1.04
Donald McCain	24	143	16.78%	58.43	-26.79	57.34	1.23	1.41
Peter Bowen	22	86	25.58%	59.55	38.84	60.47	1.93	1.64
Dianne Sayer	11	108	10.19%	45.63	-63.50	39.35	0.87	1.10
Micky Hammond	10	98	10.20%	52.00	-40.63	50.00	0.83	1.15
Martin Todhunter	10	56	17.86%	58.62	-9.63	56.25	1.46	1.46
Gordon Elliott, Ireland	8	34	23.53%	69.20	-6.68	77.94	1.96	2.41
Sam England	7	27	25.93%	58.36	49.00	57.41	2.34	1.10
Julia Brooke	6	31	19.35%	59.56	6.33	45.16	1.92	1.16
Jonjo O'Neill	6	30	20.00%	57.40	-1.00	50.00	1.36	1.50

CATTERICK BRIDGE

Trainer	Wins	Runs	Strike Rate	% Rivals Beaten	P/L	Run To Form %	Impact Value	Market Value
Donald McCain	26	153	16.99%	59.07	0.75	61.76	1.33	1.40
Sue Smith	19	81	23.46%	61.70	4.83	62.96	1.83	1.50
Micky Hammond	17	180	9.44%	47.85	-38.00	41.39	0.80	0.80
Brian Ellison	11	45	24.44%	63.67	-15.64	66.67	1.85	1.96
Sam England	10	41	24.39%	58.77	7.41	63.41	1.79	1.29
Rebecca Menzies	10	41	24.39%	61.17	39.21	60.98	1.95	1.06
Dan Skelton	9	39	23.08%	55.76	-16.36	60.26	1.77	2.47
Philip Kirby	8	66	12.12%	50.07	3.88	49.24	1.16	0.78
Jonjo O'Neill	7	34	20.59%	56.69	26.38	51.47	1.72	1.70
Jamie Snowden	6	12	50.00%	80.42	2.53	75.00	3.17	1.85

CHELTENHAM

Trainer	Wins	Runs	Strike Rate	% Rivals Beaten	P/L	Run To Form %	Impact Value	Market Value
Nicky Henderson	49	374	13.10%	53.45	-83.11	60.70	1.45	1.70
Paul Nicholls	33	323	10.22%	52.39	-52.16	58.51	1.07	1.42
W. P. Mullins, Ireland	32	299	10.70%	56.02	-19.99	66.39	1.60	1.86
Gordon Elliott, Ireland	31	209	14.83%	61.23	60.30	67.46	2.26	1.95
Colin Tizzard	26	252	10.32%	48.83	-88.77	56.75	1.06	1.16
Nigel Twiston-Davies	26	260	10.00%	52.46	-84.43	58.08	1.09	1.22
Fergal O'Brien	20	158	12.66%	57.06	28.25	63.61	1.48	1.18
Philip Hobbs	18	213	8.45%	53.69	-101.23	57.04	0.98	1.48
Dan Skelton	18	223	8.07%	53.34	-67.29	61.88	0.90	1.24
Alan King	15	159	9.43%	49.45	-43.04	59.43	1.13	1.19

CHEPSTOW

Trainer	Wins	Runs	Strike Rate	% Rivals Beaten	P/L	Run To Form %	Impact Value	Market Value
Paul Nicholls	36	160	22.50%	63.96	-19.35	71.88	2.01	2.31
Evan Williams	32	218	14.68%	55.21	70.62	56.65	1.40	1.33
Philip Hobbs	31	152	20.39%	57.34	0.30	59.54	2.06	1.98
Colin Tizzard	27	211	12.80%	55.13	-71.23	55.69	1.19	1.49
Nigel Twiston-Davies	17	102	16.67%	60.28	-10.57	59.80	1.65	1.55
Venetia Williams	16	121	13.22%	54.58	-39.69	56.20	1.18	1.30
Tom George	16	78	20.51%	56.62	-13.79	60.26	2.01	1.60
David Pipe	13	95	13.68%	58.59	-15.27	60.00	1.39	1.49
Neil Mulholland	12	101	11.88%	49.68	-16.80	48.02	1.29	1.00
Fergal O'Brien	11	68	16.18%	59.14	-14.00	61.76	1.42	1.58

DONCASTER

Trainer	Wins	Runs	Strike Rate	% Rivals Beaten	P/L	Run To Form %	Impact Value	Market Value
Nicky Henderson	25	84	29.76%	67.33	-8.70	69.64	2.23	2.77
Alan King	23	126	18.25%	58.81	-17.62	60.32	1.38	1.64
Dan Skelton	17	109	15.60%	51.70	-39.55	52.75	1.20	1.35
Paul Nicholls	17	68	25.00%	54.95	-14.45	63.24	1.58	1.83
Ben Pauling	12	54	22.22%	47.55	37.53	48.15	1.74	1.43
Charlie Longsdon	12	97	12.37%	51.77	-5.55	63.40	1.05	1.10
Jonjo O'Neill	10	95	10.53%	50.87	-28.39	48.95	1.03	1.19
Ian Williams	10	75	13.33%	47.18	-7.83	50.67	1.07	1.02
Emma Lavelle	10	40	25.00%	62.34	4.82	63.75	2.19	1.66
Donald McCain	10	74	13.51%	52.38	-5.67	51.35	1.02	1.05

EXETER

Trainer	Wins	Runs	Strike Rate	% Rivals Beaten	P/L	Run To Form %	Impact Value	Market Value
Philip Hobbs	44	218	20.18%	60.88	-69.81	67.20	1.65	2.02
Paul Nicholls	36	126	28.57%	66.37	-28.76	69.44	2.02	2.46
Colin Tizzard	30	195	15.38%	58.37	-66.95	60.51	1.32	1.53
Harry Fry	29	87	33.33%	70.88	46.53	75.29	2.86	2.76
David Pipe	20	184	10.87%	50.88	-52.15	52.45	1.03	1.33
Evan Williams	20	96	20.83%	50.37	35.88	52.08	1.54	1.19
Venetia Williams	15	78	19.23%	54.44	4.78	57.05	1.67	1.47
Susan Gardner	13	116	11.21%	47.64	-36.13	41.81	0.99	0.86
Alan King	10	64	15.63%	60.78	-26.65	64.84	1.38	2.03
Emma Lavelle	10	51	19.61%	59.37	10.50	65.69	1.90	1.77

FAKENHAM

Trainer	Wins	Runs	Strike Rate	% Rivals Beaten	P/L	Run To Form %	Impact Value	Market Value
Olly Murphy	28	117	23.93%	61.60	-6.47	66.24	1.41	1.54
Lucy Wadham	18	65	27.69%	60.39	17.38	69.23	1.87	1.40
Neil Mulholland	16	53	30.19%	58.72	7.51	69.81	1.95	1.62
Dan Skelton	15	63	23.81%	62.30	-11.02	65.87	1.41	1.61
Christian Williams	13	35	37.14%	65.66	11.57	71.43	2.38	1.62
Stuart Edmunds	11	31	35.48%	63.74	39.67	74.19	2.25	1.52
Nicky Henderson	11	40	27.50%	59.95	-17.91	62.50	1.63	2.63
Neil King	10	79	12.66%	46.90	-15.83	58.23	0.81	1.02
Paul Nicholls	8	29	27.59%	56.04	-6.62	58.62	1.31	1.91
Charlie Mann	7	30	23.33%	47.19	12.00	58.33	1.47	1.08

FFOS LAS

Trainer	Wins	Runs	Strike Rate	% Rivals Beaten	P/L	Run To Form %	Impact Value	Market Value
Evan Williams	42	298	14.09%	51.85	-64.62	52.01	1.07	1.19
Peter Bowen	31	213	14.55%	50.28	-77.04	47.89	1.08	1.21
Nigel Twiston-Davies	26	128	20.31%	60.34	5.09	61.33	1.58	1.63
Rebecca Curtis	20	88	22.73%	55.77	-5.13	55.68	1.80	1.61
Tim Vaughan	13	130	10.00%	42.94	-27.50	43.46	0.78	1.02
Nicky Henderson	13	36	36.11%	62.21	-4.51	61.11	2.62	2.76
Debra Hamer	12	77	15.58%	49.39	-9.63	44.16	1.25	1.05
David Rees	11	103	10.68%	50.26	-18.38	45.15	0.89	1.11
David Pipe	10	83	12.05%	55.35	-51.43	56.63	0.99	1.73
Colin Tizzard	10	32	31.25%	62.11	33.73	65.63	2.54	1.55

FONTWELL PARK

Trainer	Wins	Runs	Strike Rate	% Rivals Beaten	P/L	Run To Form %	Impact Value	Market Value
Gary Moore	65	352	18.47%	54.25	19.85	57.10	1.32	1.36
Neil Mulholland	41	197	20.81%	58.22	29.97	58.88	1.41	1.28
Paul Nicholls	39	92	42.39%	73.74	18.73	78.80	2.32	2.19
Chris Gordon	32	240	13.33%	52.22	-5.66	53.96	1.02	1.21
Anthony Honeyball	30	89	33.71%	67.85	33.09	67.98	2.18	1.84
Colin Tizzard	25	130	19.23%	56.00	-34.17	57.31	1.29	1.53
Dan Skelton	19	101	18.81%	59.11	-27.86	61.39	1.29	1.65
Philip Hobbs	18	69	26.09%	59.96	-18.64	65.94	1.76	2.23
Seamus Mullins	17	161	10.56%	45.98	-40.08	48.45	0.80	0.93
Alan King	16	57	28.07%	63.39	2.77	65.79	2.13	2.22

HAYDOCK PARK

Trainer	Wins	Runs	Strike Rate	% Rivals Beaten	P/L	Run To Form %	Impact Value	Market Value
Nigel Twiston-Davies	20	108	18.52%	56.72	-14.74	58.80	1.49	1.27
Sue Smith	18	109	16.51%	62.30	15.62	65.60	1.24	1.34
Paul Nicholls	14	65	21.54%	58.04	-22.38	73.85	1.50	1.63
Donald McCain	13	96	13.54%	52.25	-33.22	56.25	0.98	0.93
Venetia Williams	13	64	20.31%	53.33	66.71	50.78	1.52	1.58
Nicky Henderson	13	46	28.26%	59.15	3.74	66.30	1.84	1.74
David Pipe	9	59	15.25%	54.41	22.83	52.54	1.47	1.39
Tom George	9	46	19.57%	50.50	-5.17	54.35	1.66	1.57
Jonjo O'Neill	7	46	15.22%	44.21	-3.25	50.00	1.28	1.36
Dan Skelton	7	75	9.33%	48.99	-38.13	48.67	0.74	1.29

HEREFORD

Trainer	Wins	Runs	Strike Rate	% Rivals Beaten	P/L	Run To Form %	Impact Value	Market Value
Venetia Williams	16	80	20.00%	45.99	8.23	47.50	1.72	1.30
Dan Skelton	12	48	25.00%	60.36	-0.48	62.50	2.16	2.18
Philip Hobbs	8	35	22.86%	67.74	-10.86	78.57	1.81	2.30
Kim Bailey	7	33	21.21%	65.62	0.82	69.70	1.88	1.80
Warren Greatrex	7	32	21.88%	73.18	-10.37	71.88	2.00	2.42
Evan Williams	7	80	8.75%	46.12	-40.10	45.63	0.74	1.12
Henry Oliver	7	54	12.96%	52.91	0.00	46.30	1.23	1.03
Alan King	6	21	28.57%	62.29	6.53	54.76	2.57	2.38
Neil Mulholland	6	30	20.00%	58.77	-5.21	65.00	1.89	1.58
Alastair Ralph	6	24	25.00%	64.32	18.85	64.58	2.62	1.24

HEXHAM

Trainer	Wins	Runs	Strike Rate	% Rivals Beaten	P/L	Run To Form %	Impact Value	Market Value
Lucinda Russell	31	222	13.96%	55.83	38.17	55.86	1.16	1.27
Micky Hammond	26	203	12.81%	50.41	-41.62	45.57	1.13	1.12
Maurice Barnes	22	148	14.86%	52.71	-21.00	53.04	1.25	1.11
Nicky Richards	17	52	32.69%	60.44	2.75	59.62	2.78	2.41
George Bewley	13	88	14.77%	48.05	3.75	40.91	1.31	0.91
Mark Walford	12	75	16.00%	61.57	-19.10	60.00	1.42	1.48
Stuart Coltherd	11	88	12.50%	54.05	-12.00	50.57	1.13	1.37
Martin Todhunter	11	84	13.10%	53.07	-9.00	52.38	1.06	1.15
James Ewart	11	60	18.33%	55.91	-3.00	51.67	1.69	1.37
Brian Ellison	11	58	18.97%	60.73	-1.80	64.66	1.57	1.64

HUNTINGDON

Trainer	Wins	Runs	Strike Rate	% Rivals Beaten	P/L	Run To Form %	Impact Value	Market Value
Nicky Henderson	30	111	27.03%	67.64	-37.11	70.72	2.19	2.65
Dan Skelton	29	168	17.26%	59.90	-58.84	60.12	1.43	1.81
Jonjo O'Neill	22	117	18.80%	55.87	6.58	55.98	1.70	1.58
Kim Bailey	22	117	18.80%	54.02	8.68	60.68	1.59	1.46
Alan King	18	108	16.67%	67.59	-1.65	69.91	1.41	2.13
Fergal O'Brien	16	61	26.23%	65.02	55.58	66.39	2.13	1.61
Ben Pauling	15	90	16.67%	52.48	38.55	46.67	1.45	1.53
Gary Moore	12	114	10.53%	52.05	-26.00	50.44	0.91	1.25
Olly Murphy	11	39	28.21%	62.55	-9.23	70.51	2.23	1.89
Charlie Longsdon	11	107	10.28%	45.22	-34.25	48.60	0.88	1.03

KELSO

Trainer	Wins	Runs	Strike Rate	% Rivals Beaten	P/L	Run To Form %	Impact Value	Market Value
Lucinda Russell	40	262	15.27%	55.23	-27.88	54.39	1.21	1.11
N. W. Alexander	27	194	13.92%	48.70	-5.24	51.29	1.11	1.04
Nicky Richards	25	125	20.00%	59.86	3.52	62.40	1.43	1.78
Donald McCain	21	146	14.38%	51.40	-34.66	56.51	1.03	1.41
Sandy Thomson	19	116	16.38%	58.42	46.23	62.50	1.25	1.27
Keith Dalgleish	17	70	24.29%	59.15	18.64	65.00	1.84	1.91
Rose Dobbin	14	125	11.20%	52.78	-35.81	52.00	0.97	1.16
James Ewart	12	96	12.50%	51.42	-5.13	50.52	1.01	1.23
Micky Hammond	11	86	12.79%	47.76	-31.42	44.19	1.01	1.07
Iain Jardine	10	65	15.38%	55.31	-16.08	53.08	1.20	1.33

KEMPTON PARK

Trainer	Wins	Runs	Strike Rate	% Rivals Beaten	P/L	Run To Form %	Impact Value	Market Value
Nicky Henderson	63	239	26.36%	62.12	-34.60	63.60	2.04	2.19
Paul Nicholls	47	227	20.70%	58.91	-38.43	67.18	1.40	1.62
Alan King	26	183	14.21%	54.56	-61.91	60.38	1.18	1.56
Harry Fry	15	80	18.75%	56.86	-13.88	56.88	1.68	1.75
Chris Gordon	12	85	14.12%	54.54	-18.40	51.76	1.27	1.23
Nigel Twiston-Davies	12	81	14.81%	53.76	0.43	51.23	1.27	1.11
Tom George	11	71	15.49%	55.05	5.00	66.90	1.21	1.31
Philip Hobbs	11	100	11.00%	57.15	-60.80	62.50	0.90	1.52
Ben Pauling	11	53	20.75%	54.71	31.44	64.15	1.96	1.41
Colin Tizzard	11	80	13.75%	56.97	22.35	56.88	1.17	1.23

LEICESTER

Trainer	Wins	Runs	Strike Rate	% Rivals Beaten	P/L	Run To Form %	Impact Value	Market Value
Tom George	14	37	37.84%	73.15	23.37	81.08	2.54	1.66
Dan Skelton	13	42	30.95%	66.45	12.42	70.24	2.02	1.66
Nigel Twiston-Davies	12	56	21.43%	62.20	19.71	66.07	1.43	1.26
Caroline Bailey	10	38	26.32%	55.72	4.99	57.89	1.66	1.26
Philip Hobbs	9	21	42.86%	79.21	12.25	80.95	2.87	2.38
Fergal O'Brien	8	36	22.22%	55.98	16.57	56.94	1.51	1.39
Robin Dickin	8	35	22.86%	57.47	21.63	58.57	1.63	1.16
David Pipe	7	27	25.93%	57.44	1.32	61.11	1.44	1.57
Venetia Williams	7	28	25.00%	59.14	-6.75	55.36	1.46	1.91
Gary Moore	7	21	33.33%	61.15	4.92	57.14	2.41	1.78

LINGFIELD PARK

Trainer	Wins	Runs	Strike Rate	% Rivals Beaten	P/L	Run To Form %	Impact Value	Market Value
Gary Moore	12	115	10.43%	49.60	-43.50	53.91	0.77	1.16
Seamus Mullins	10	59	16.95%	49.49	51.38	44.92	1.37	0.84
Zoe Davison	8	45	17.78%	52.78	-3.88	48.89	1.24	0.77
Warren Greatrex	7	30	23.33%	55.47	-13.38	60.00	1.67	2.11
Chris Gordon	7	45	15.56%	55.33	-13.65	53.33	1.10	1.23
Lucy Wadham	7	22	31.82%	70.40	40.19	72.73	2.59	1.64
Dan Skelton	6	24	25.00%	66.67	2.25	64.58	1.82	2.01
Anna Newton-Smith	5	27	18.52%	49.47	7.50	38.89	1.56	1.20
Martin Keighley	5	18	27.78%	57.06	10.17	55.56	2.22	1.32
Emma Lavelle	5	19	26.32%	68.66	7.50	65.79	2.26	1.54

LUDLOW

Trainer	Wins	Runs	Strike Rate	% Rivals Beaten	P/L	Run To Form %	Impact Value	Market Value
Nicky Henderson	29	93	31.18%	66.31	-2.41	68.28	2.53	2.62
Dan Skelton	27	126	21.43%	63.96	-31.68	61.51	1.79	2.21
Philip Hobbs	27	111	24.32%	65.85	4.79	69.82	1.94	2.14
Evan Williams	20	197	10.15%	48.85	-86.76	52.03	0.77	1.19
Henry Daly	20	109	18.35%	59.40	-34.12	59.17	1.60	1.40
Kim Bailey	18	107	16.82%	56.99	-27.06	59.81	1.41	1.77
Paul Nicholls	17	58	29.31%	60.95	-5.60	68.10	1.89	2.22
Nigel Twiston-Davies	17	132	12.88%	53.64	-60.09	55.30	1.09	1.44
Tom George	16	105	15.24%	64.36	-23.09	65.71	1.23	1.44
Venetia Williams	14	101	13.86%	57.12	-27.63	59.41	1.22	1.32

MARKET RASEN

Trainer	Wins	Runs	Strike Rate	% Rivals Beaten	P/L	Run To Form %	Impact Value	Market Value
Dan Skelton	61	253	24.11%	62.52	-21.10	63.83	1.81	1.97
Olly Murphy	27	125	21.60%	64.73	-16.06	66.00	1.70	1.82
Dr Richard Newland	23	74	31.08%	65.15	33.11	66.89	2.56	2.17
Fergal O'Brien	22	112	19.64%	55.64	11.17	61.16	1.47	1.57
Nicky Henderson	21	75	28.00%	62.42	-14.64	68.00	2.07	2.31
Jonjo O'Neill	20	155	12.90%	49.57	-62.98	53.87	1.00	1.37
Brian Ellison	20	121	16.53%	49.66	-20.38	54.13	1.26	1.30
Alan King	18	95	18.95%	57.97	-9.30	62.63	1.46	1.60
Peter Bowen	13	77	16.88%	51.50	-9.08	58.44	1.40	1.46
Nigel Twiston-Davies	13	63	20.63%	56.33	23.23	60.32	1.66	1.59

MUSSELBURGH

Trainer	Wins	Runs	Strike Rate	% Rivals Beaten	P/L	Run To Form %	Impact Value	Market Value
Lucinda Russell	33	255	12.94%	51.05	-40.68	50.59	1.02	1.06
Keith Dalgleish	28	104	26.92%	60.15	0.23	62.50	1.95	1.70
Donald McCain	20	125	16.00%	59.40	-18.97	62.00	1.14	1.38
Paul Nicholls	17	39	43.59%	70.79	13.95	75.64	2.76	2.18
Sandy Thomson	16	79	20.25%	58.04	0.38	62.66	1.53	1.53
Iain Jardine	12	108	11.11%	54.14	-24.43	56.94	0.88	1.14
Jim Goldie	9	87	10.34%	48.47	-28.84	45.40	0.86	0.96
Tim Vaughan	8	53	15.09%	55.43	-13.93	60.38	1.08	1.36
James Ewart	8	65	12.31%	48.15	0.25	45.38	1.04	1.21
N. W. Alexander	7	74	9.46%	52.18	-28.00	45.27	0.82	0.96

NEWBURY

Trainer	Wins	Runs	Strike Rate	% Rivals Beaten	P/L	Run To Form %	Impact Value	Market Value
Nicky Henderson	52	216	24.07%	61.80	-7.76	69.44	2.31	2.21
Philip Hobbs	23	135	17.04%	59.19	52.92	65.56	1.58	1.63
Colin Tizzard	21	122	17.21%	59.47	-19.56	59.84	1.50	1.45
Paul Nicholls	19	141	13.48%	55.09	-6.18	62.41	1.09	1.52
Alan King	15	166	9.04%	59.36	-89.07	65.96	0.88	1.47
Ben Pauling	12	65	18.46%	51.17	-2.14	53.08	1.74	1.46
Warren Greatrex	12	78	15.38%	53.88	-20.75	52.56	1.38	1.11
Dan Skelton	10	113	8.85%	51.59	-51.00	53.98	0.87	1.28
Harry Fry	9	66	13.64%	53.44	-28.92	59.09	1.37	2.34
Nigel Twiston-Davies	8	87	9.20%	50.25	-44.09	50.57	0.91	1.23

NEWCASTLE

Trainer	Wins	Runs	Strike Rate	% Rivals Beaten	P/L	Run To Form %	Impact Value	Market Value
Sue Smith	21	100	21.00%	62.61	7.99	67.50	1.62	1.61
N. W. Alexander	15	100	15.00%	49.66	-16.55	52.50	1.14	1.09
Nicky Richards	15	72	20.83%	60.53	1.27	59.72	1.59	1.96
Brian Ellison	15	60	25.00%	63.43	-11.15	67.50	1.73	1.89
Micky Hammond	13	97	13.40%	45.35	-13.43	44.85	0.94	0.94
Philip Kirby	12	74	16.22%	53.69	-13.08	54.05	1.26	1.08
Sandy Thomson	11	53	20.75%	56.10	19.28	64.15	1.43	1.39
Lucinda Russell	10	94	10.64%	49.74	-52.00	50.00	0.82	1.05
Keith Dalgleish	10	36	27.78%	66.45	48.43	65.28	2.23	1.99
James Ewart	8	66	12.12%	52.19	-32.50	46.97	0.96	1.37

NEWTON ABBOT

Trainer	Wins	Runs	Strike Rate	% Rivals Beaten	P/L	Run To Form %	Impact Value	Market Value
Paul Nicholls	41	142	28.87%	63.42	-41.26	65.49	1.58	2.09
Philip Hobbs	26	134	19.40%	59.09	-34.96	64.55	1.50	1.91
Colin Tizzard	26	145	17.93%	58.09	-7.75	56.55	1.25	1.42
Tim Vaughan	18	95	18.95%	54.01	17.45	52.63	1.76	1.35
Jeremy Scott	15	89	16.85%	55.62	-9.50	48.31	1.42	1.24
David Pipe	13	138	9.42%	48.50	-51.50	50.36	0.78	1.35
Dan Skelton	12	78	15.38%	55.90	-43.52	55.77	1.20	2.48
Neil Mulholland	12	118	10.17%	49.82	-20.88	46.19	0.84	1.35
Emma Lavelle	10	39	25.64%	52.52	39.75	56.41	1.97	1.30
Harry Fry	10	51	19.61%	62.50	-15.25	70.59	1.60	1.93

PERTH

Trainer	Wins	Runs	Strike Rate	% Rivals Beaten	P/L	Run To Form %	Impact Value	Market Value
Gordon Elliott, Ireland	71	269	26.39%	66.62	-59.32	69.52	1.77	2.08
Lucinda Russell	30	337	8.90%	47.27	-99.59	46.74	0.67	0.89
Fergal O'Brien	22	80	27.50%	57.81	19.50	61.25	1.90	1.63
Nicky Richards	21	147	14.29%	54.09	-27.04	57.82	1.13	1.41
Donald McCain	19	75	25.33%	51.85	25.23	61.33	1.68	1.19
Lisa Harrison	17	156	10.90%	45.87	-46.92	46.15	0.84	0.90
Nigel Twiston-Davies	15	82	18.29%	54.38	-34.16	54.27	1.29	1.78
Keith Dalgleish	12	42	28.57%	62.05	-2.76	66.67	1.91	1.53
Peter Bowen	11	28	39.29%	70.75	15.87	76.79	2.70	1.93
Stuart Crawford, Ireland	10	117	8.55%	44.81	-65.65	45.30	0.66	0.95

PLUMPTON

Trainer	Wins	Runs	Strike Rate	% Rivals Beaten	P/L	Run To Form %	Impact Value	Market Value
Gary Moore	53	334	15.87%	53.97	-97.06	57.19	1.14	1.47
Chris Gordon	34	176	19.32%	56.76	17.77	59.94	1.47	1.44
Anthony Honeyball	16	65	24.62%	57.06	-16.04	66.92	1.74	2.05
Sheena West	15	88	17.05%	54.35	53.75	51.14	1.42	0.97
Neil King	14	66	21.21%	55.31	-17.76	56.82	1.35	1.34
Zoe Davison	14	109	12.84%	48.03	1.60	41.28	0.99	0.66
Colin Tizzard	14	84	16.67%	54.31	-31.96	60.71	1.23	1.40
Alan King	14	47	29.79%	65.87	-15.71	78.72	2.15	2.68
Seamus Mullins	12	118	10.17%	48.87	-17.04	43.22	0.74	0.98
Dan Skelton	11	36	30.56%	69.34	-8.88	66.67	2.39	2.34

SANDOWN PARK

Trainer	Wins	Runs	Strike Rate	% Rivals Beaten	P/L	Run To Form %	Impact Value	Market Value
Nicky Henderson	39	145	26.90%	62.09	-8.79	65.52	2.17	1.97
Gary Moore	22	150	14.67%	46.02	-3.18	51.33	1.11	0.98
Paul Nicholls	18	169	10.65%	51.63	-67.43	63.61	0.80	1.23
Philip Hobbs	15	93	16.13%	58.75	-18.65	59.68	1.42	1.52
Nigel Twiston-Davies	13	63	20.63%	52.74	50.71	55.56	1.91	1.40
Alan King	11	59	18.64%	59.88	8.46	71.19	1.60	1.50
Fergal O'Brien	10	39	25.64%	59.30	20.13	61.54	2.48	1.52
Colin Tizzard	10	86	11.63%	48.65	-48.20	54.65	1.01	1.33
Venetia Williams	8	83	9.64%	52.50	-36.25	60.24	0.84	1.29
Charlie Longsdon	6	58	10.34%	54.00	15.75	56.03	1.01	0.94

SEDGEFIELD

Trainer	Wins	Runs	Strike Rate	% Rivals Beaten	P/L	Run To Form %	Impact Value	Market Value
Donald McCain	44	264	16.67%	55.33	-23.99	57.77	1.12	1.41
Brian Ellison	40	157	25.48%	62.79	-13.66	67.83	1.72	1.56
Micky Hammond	36	295	12.20%	46.48	-116.12	42.54	0.90	1.01
Sue Smith	27	172	15.70%	57.69	-41.25	60.47	1.15	1.42
Neil Mulholland	19	45	42.22%	65.22	16.37	71.11	2.67	2.09
Philip Kirby	16	95	16.84%	55.89	6.08	52.63	1.26	1.28
Sam England	16	84	19.05%	54.16	3.40	54.76	1.43	1.19
Chris Grant	14	148	9.46%	46.41	-17.50	41.55	0.74	0.83
Dan Skelton	14	62	22.58%	65.46	-15.65	66.13	1.55	2.28
Evan Williams	13	40	32.50%	63.35	17.08	62.50	2.09	1.65

SOUTHWELL

Trainer	Wins	Runs	Strike Rate	% Rivals Beaten	P/L	Run To Form %	Impact Value	Market Value
Dan Skelton	44	193	22.80%	64.67	-44.47	68.65	1.74	2.13
Jonjo O'Neill	23	161	14.29%	56.92	-44.30	57.14	1.13	1.41
Nicky Henderson	18	53	33.96%	68.58	-6.45	75.47	2.21	2.50
Tom George	18	77	23.38%	67.05	-16.42	74.03	1.66	1.89
Caroline Bailey	16	88	18.18%	58.46	0.88	56.82	1.46	1.44
Harry Whittington	14	49	28.57%	66.85	51.09	67.35	2.43	1.62
Tim Vaughan	13	100	13.00%	52.55	-11.38	52.00	1.05	1.10
Ben Pauling	13	61	21.31%	57.76	-3.65	63.11	1.81	1.69
Alan King	13	54	24.07%	67.30	-18.53	67.59	1.67	1.92
Dr Richard Newland	13	40	32.50%	72.33	-5.06	68.75	2.29	2.45

STRATFORD-ON-AVON

Trainer	Wins	Runs	Strike Rate	% Rivals Beaten	P/L	Run To Form %	Impact Value	Market Value
Dan Skelton	29	160	18.13%	60.09	-62.64	62.50	1.37	1.99
Tom George	17	66	25.76%	60.61	26.07	61.36	1.95	1.84
Philip Hobbs	16	60	26.67%	58.07	27.65	64.17	1.96	1.58
Nigel Twiston-Davies	16	86	18.60%	54.22	-12.84	51.16	1.42	1.45
Dr Richard Newland	16	51	31.37%	62.83	-15.27	60.78	2.08	2.20
Warren Greatrex	15	56	26.79%	58.29	12.99	57.14	1.98	2.17
Donald McCain	14	62	22.58%	60.16	28.38	54.84	1.58	1.26
Neil Mulholland	14	84	16.67%	54.27	19.00	52.38	1.30	1.27
Olly Murphy	13	75	17.33%	51.04	-31.88	54.00	1.31	1.66
Alan King	12	45	26.67%	75.37	-6.06	75.56	2.11	2.02

TAUNTON

Trainer	Wins	Runs	Strike Rate	% Rivals Beaten	P/L	Run To Form %	Impact Value	Market Value
Paul Nicholls	51	188	27.13%	70.25	-36.97	71.54	2.12	2.83
Philip Hobbs	20	141	14.18%	64.68	-59.38	71.63	1.28	1.77
Harry Fry	20	85	23.53%	67.72	-19.86	73.53	2.06	2.29
Colin Tizzard	19	143	13.29%	51.39	-9.48	46.15	1.16	1.34
Jeremy Scott	15	69	21.74%	59.68	38.10	57.97	2.08	1.56
Nicky Henderson	13	35	37.14%	76.17	2.62	77.14	2.69	2.50
David Pipe	12	143	8.39%	51.60	-66.64	46.85	0.78	1.25
Evan Williams	12	126	9.52%	46.80	-54.58	43.25	0.82	1.01
Neil Mulholland	12	103	11.65%	48.41	-9.00	38.35	1.15	1.03
Dan Skelton	10	63	15.87%	48.28	-28.33	57.94	1.35	1.53

UTTOXETER

Trainer	Wins	Runs	Strike Rate	% Rivals Beaten	P/L	Run To Form %	Impact Value	Market Value
Dan Skelton	74	261	28.35%	65.91	18.58	64.75	2.51	2.22
Jonjo O'Neill	31	246	12.60%	47.91	-62.06	48.78	1.15	1.37
Dr Richard Newland	24	78	30.77%	72.08	8.35	72.44	2.47	2.46
David Pipe	21	129	16.28%	56.58	5.36	58.53	1.52	1.63
Philip Hobbs	20	111	18.02%	56.97	-46.26	59.01	1.54	1.76
Nigel Twiston-Davies	20	147	13.61%	57.33	-57.33	55.44	1.24	1.54
Nicky Henderson	20	77	25.97%	65.46	-19.34	64.94	1.97	2.39
Charlie Longsdon	20	117	17.09%	54.17	-10.42	58.55	1.52	1.43
Warren Greatrex	18	77	23.38%	60.44	0.09	62.34	1.95	1.78
Fergal O'Brien	17	96	17.71%	59.75	36.43	61.46	1.55	1.57

WARWICK

Trainer	Wins	Runs	Strike Rate	% Rivals Beaten	P/L	Run To Form %	Impact Value	Market Value
Dan Skelton	57	258	22.09%	58.95	-63.25	62.98	1.83	2.02
Nicky Henderson	31	107	28.97%	66.97	4.24	66.82	2.47	2.52
Alan King	29	144	20.14%	67.32	-61.73	67.01	1.85	2.27
Jonjo O'Neill	28	172	16.28%	51.99	53.66	50.00	1.53	1.18
Philip Hobbs	25	113	22.12%	65.08	1.71	63.72	1.93	2.03
Nigel Twiston-Davies	20	180	11.11%	56.09	-89.64	56.39	0.93	1.32
Charlie Longsdon	13	109	11.93%	52.90	-34.46	55.50	1.05	1.27
Neil Mulholland	13	59	22.03%	53.77	6.42	52.54	1.58	1.22
Kim Bailey	12	82	14.63%	58.41	0.50	57.93	1.31	1.28
Jeremy Scott	11	59	18.64%	52.76	27.24	55.93	1.71	1.23

WETHERBY

Trainer	Wins	Runs	Strike Rate	% Rivals Beaten	P/L	Run To Form %	Impact Value	Market Value
Dan Skelton	41	144	28.47%	66.22	3.96	70.49	2.18	2.06
Philip Kirby	29	179	16.20%	48.21	9.56	49.16	1.47	0.98
Micky Hammond	22	290	7.59%	44.68	-57.00	44.31	0.65	0.77
Nigel Twiston-Davies	16	72	22.22%	57.26	-11.42	65.28	1.63	1.68
Sue Smith	16	176	9.09%	52.27	-112.06	54.83	0.73	1.28
Kim Bailey	13	44	29.55%	69.07	4.77	75.00	2.18	2.07
Nicky Richards	13	53	24.53%	56.94	49.13	61.32	1.94	1.59
Rose Dobbin	12	76	15.79%	56.17	0.46	55.92	1.36	1.11
Warren Greatrex	12	60	20.00%	58.22	-19.99	58.33	1.52	2.09
Brian Ellison	11	78	14.10%	55.92	-25.45	58.97	1.04	1.26

WINCANTON

Trainer	Wins	Runs	Strike Rate	% Rivals Beaten	P/L	Run To Form %	Impact Value	Market Value
Paul Nicholls	100	292	34.25%	67.50	7.50	71.92	2.42	2.67
Colin Tizzard	38	274	13.87%	56.47	-29.46	56.93	1.16	1.38
Philip Hobbs	20	164	12.20%	56.33	-52.13	58.84	1.11	1.50
Harry Fry	16	92	17.39%	55.65	-6.06	58.15	1.46	1.83
Jeremy Scott	15	118	12.71%	53.75	-15.63	55.93	1.09	1.09
Neil Mulholland	15	173	8.67%	52.63	-52.65	50.29	0.69	1.11
Emma Lavelle	13	66	19.70%	62.43	23.38	66.67	1.77	1.51
Venetia Williams	10	60	16.67%	55.35	-7.75	58.33	1.31	1.27
Anthony Honeyball	9	55	16.36%	58.56	-17.18	53.64	1.32	1.50
Alan King	8	74	10.81%	60.27	-45.11	62.16	0.94	1.72

WOLVERHAMPTON

Trainer	Wins	Runs	Strike Rate	% Rivals Beaten	P/L	Run To Form %	Impact Value	Market Value
Dan Skelton	2	5	40.00%	69.43	1.13	50.00	3.08	1.93
Ed de Giles	1	2	50.00%	75.00	15.00	50.00	5.96	0.40
Paul Nicholls	1	3	33.33%	88.57	-1.27	66.67	2.79	3.72
Ben Pauling	1	2	50.00%	66.67	27.00	50.00	5.65	0.37
Harry Whittington	1	2	50.00%	88.89	1.50	75.00	4.44	1.81
Neil King	1	4	25.00%	62.50	0.00	62.50	2.09	0.85
Aytach Sadik	0	1	0.00%	0.00	-1.00	0.00	0.00	0.01
Brian Ellison	0	2	0.00%	74.17	-2.00	50.00	0.00	1.35
Alan King	0	3	0.00%	42.41	-3.00	0.00	0.00	2.48
Charlie Mann	0	1	0.00%	83.33	-1.00	100.00	0.00	0.54

WORCESTER

Trainer	Wins	Runs	Strike Rate	% Rivals Beaten	P/L	Run To Form %	Impact Value	Market Value
Jonjo O'Neill	36	219	16.44%	55.19	-42.92	57.53	1.36	1.45
Dan Skelton	34	179	18.99%	59.23	-40.77	58.10	1.51	1.90
Philip Hobbs	33	116	28.45%	62.98	67.85	60.34	2.23	1.87
Dr Richard Newland	27	92	29.35%	70.23	-4.19	75.54	2.22	2.18
David Pipe	25	148	16.89%	56.15	20.75	63.18	1.42	1.40
Nigel Twiston-Davies	24	102	23.53%	59.88	11.28	59.80	1.95	1.47
Peter Bowen	23	111	20.72%	59.25	53.38	62.16	1.74	1.50
Neil Mulholland	23	176	13.07%	52.32	-74.50	52.56	1.07	1.28
Nicky Henderson	22	89	24.72%	63.16	-17.14	67.98	1.83	2.24
Alan King	15	63	23.81%	67.28	-15.30	71.43	2.04	2.12

INDEX